SECOND EDITION
UPDATED INFORMATION

MAQS QUILTS:

The Founders Collection

This publication has been developed by the MUSEUM OF THE AMERICAN QUILTER'S SOCIETY (MAQS), Paducah, KY, in cooperation with the AMERICAN QUILTER'S SOCIETY (AQS). Publication is supported in part by contributions from the Phileona Foundation, and FRIENDS OF MAQS across the country. MAQS educational programs are supported in part by the Kentucky Arts Council.

EDITOR: VICTORIA A. FAORO
GRAPHIC DESIGN: KAY BLACKBURN SMITH
COVER DESIGN: ELAINE WILSON
PHOTOGRAPHY: CHARLES R. LYNCH, RICHARD WALKER

Library of Congress Cataloging-in-Publication Data
MAQS.
        MAQS quilts: the founder's collection / by Museum of the American Quilter's Society; Victoria A. Faoro, editor.
        p.   cm.
        ISBN 1-57432-780-1
        1. Quilts--United States--History--20th century--Catalogs.
2. Quilts--Kentucky--Paducah--Catalogs. 3. MAQS--Catalogs.
I. Faoro, Victoria. II. Title.
NK9112 .M35 2001
746.46'0973'07476995--dc21
                        20001001622

Additional copies of this book may be purchased at the MAQS Bookstore, 215 Jefferson St., Paducah, KY 42001, or online at www.quiltmuseum.org. Copies can also be ordered from the American Quilter's Society, PO Box 3290, Paducah, KY 42002-3290, or online at www.AmericanQuilter.com.

PHOTO CREDITS_____

Exhibit photos by Richard Walker, Schenevus, NY, unless otherwise noted.

All quilts photographed by Richard Walker and Charles R. Lynch.

All quiltmaker photos provided by the artists.

SECOND EDITION
UPDATED INFORMATION

MAQS QUILTS:

The Founders Collection

MUSEUM OF THE AMERICAN QUILTER'S SOCIETY
PADUCAH, KENTUCKY

Close Up_____

The Museum of the American Quilter's Society (MAQS) is located in Paducah, a city of 27,000 located on the Ohio River in Western Kentucky. The museum's 30,000 square foot building is situated on the I-24 downtown loop, in the city's historic district, which includes several regional museums, theaters, antiques shops, restaurants, and other attractions. Running along the downtown is a flood wall that protects the city in times of high water on the Ohio River. In recent years the panels in this flood wall have come to depict the city's rich history through murals painted by Lafayette, Louisiana, artist Robert Dafford. Paducah's downtown and the MAQS Quilt Museum have become favorite stops for those traveling the U.S. by car, by bus, or on the steamboats navigating the Ohio and Mississippi Rivers. MAQS welcomes tens of thousands of visitors each year.

ABOVE: **Bronze marker recognizing the founding of MAQS.**

RIGHT: **Aerial view of the raising of the flag during the MAQS opening ceremony.**

PHOTO: ROBERT SHAPIRO

During the annual AQS Quilt Show & Contest in April 1991, quilters around the world gathered with MAQS founders, Bill and Meredith Schroeder, and other community members to celebrate the opening of the Museum of the American Quilter's Society in downtown Paducah, Kentucky.

Participating city and county officials, visiting state officials, the Paducah Symphony Orchestra, and Ambassador community volunteers (wearing red jackets) contributed to the excitement generated by this official opening of MAQS.

Contents

CLOSE UP_____

Bill and Meredith Schroeder have operated Schroeder Publishing since 1970, publishing the annual *Schroeder's Antiques Price Guide* and many other price guides under the Collector Book imprint.

In 1985 they founded the American Quilter's Society, an international membership organization that publishes a quarterly magazine, *American Quilter*, for its members, publishes books on quiltmaking techniques and history, and holds an international quilt show and contest each year in Paducah, Kentucky, during April. This event, annually hosting over 30,000 visitors, has resulted in Paducah's being known throughout the world as Quilt City U.S.A.® As they worked with quilters, Bill and Meredith envisioned establishing a museum that would display quilts all year long.

TOP: **Bill and Meredith Schroeder, founders of the Museum of the American Quilter's Society (MAQS).**

BOTTOM: **Banner across Broadway welcoming quilters in April.**

From the start, founders Bill and Meredith Schroeder envisioned a museum that would display quilts in such a way that they could be viewed as important works of art and at the same time carefully preserved for future generations. The museum they made a reality in 1991 provides over 13,000 square feet of exhibit space, all carefully regulated in terms of temperature and humidity, with lights filtered and adjusted to the appropriate low levels.

In addition to displays of selections from the Founders Collection, MAQS also features changing exhibits of new and antique quilts on loan from museums and private collections.

The Museum's Founders Collection and changing exhibits provide a sense of the continuing development of quiltmaking over the centuries.

LETTER FROM
The Founders

In 1987 we announced to quiltmakers that we would built a non-profit museum to honor their work. Little did we realize that this effort would have such a profound effect on the preservation and documentation of the art of quiltmaking.

Early on, quilts for the collection were acquired with private and corporate funds and later donated to the permanent collection. Purchase awards at the American Quilter's Society Annual Quilt Show and Contest assure that the collection will continually reflect the best that today's quiltmaker has to offer. This collection will truly trace the vigorous artistic renaissance in this art form.

Of particular interest, since the founding of the museum, is the proliferation of the free-hand machine quilting. When Caryl Bryer Fallert won the coveted Best of Show in the 1989 AQS Quilt Show & Contest with CORONA II: SOLAR ECLIPSE, the quilt world was astounded. Today this quilt is one of the most popular pieces in the MAQS collection.

Seven of the quilts in the museum's collection were selected to be featured in the "Best 100 Twentieth Century American Quilts." Six of the quilts in the collection are designated masterpiece quilts by the National Quilting Association.

The building of the museum and its collection have been a labor of love for us. Our rewards derive from reading the comments left by the viewers, recorded in the visitor's comment book.

It's an emotional experience for us when we walk through the galleries and see what today's quiltmakers have accomplished. There are those who say that quiltmaking is not an art form. They haven't visited the Museum of the American Quilter's Society.

Bill and Meredith Schroeder
MAQS Founders

Close Up_____

In late 1990 members of the American Quilter's Society were invited to become Friends of MAQS, making an annual contribution to support this new museum being established. Hundreds of members from around the world made donations toward program costs for this 501(c)3 non-profit organization. Over the past twelve years over 1,600 Friends of MAQS continue to provide important annual support for the museum's programs, as well as special projects. Friends enjoy special discounts and receive a pin recognizing their gift. A quarterly newsletter keeps these friends in touch with MAQS events and programs, and gifts of $100 or more are recognized on donor boards in the museum's lobby. Since 1993 MAQS has also enjoyed support from the Kentucky Arts Council.

ABOVE: **Bill and Meredith Schroeder and visiting dignitaries cut a quilted ribbon at the museum's grand opening ceremony, surrounded by community members and visiting quilters.**

CLOSE UP_____

The museum's Founders Collection includes 193 quilts, the work of 162 quiltmakers. The works in this collection were made from 1980 on.

MAQS annually welcomes over 46,000 visitors to its galleries and shop, approximately 10,000 visiting during the annual AQS Quilt Show & Contest.

On an average day at MAQS (excluding AQS Quilt Show Week), visitors will be from at least 15 different states and approximately every other day an international visitor will visit the museum.

Admission fees provide only about 17% of the museum's annual operating costs. Over 50% of the museum's expenses are supported by grants, corporate sponsorships and donations, and annual contributions from MAQS Friends, who represent all U.S. states as well as other countries.

TOP: **Featured in the MAQS lobby are stained-glass windows based on quilts. These windows by Jack Wallis, Murray, KY, were commissioned by MAQS co-founder Bill Schroeder in the late 1980s.**

BOTTOM: **Lobby stained-glass window based on BASKET OF FLOWERS, by Marzenna Krol, a quilt in the MAQS Founders Collection, page 40.**

FOREWORD BY THE FOUNDING

Executive Director

When I moved to Paducah, Kentucky, in January 1990, little did I know the excitement that awaited me at the American Quilter's Society (AQS). By the time ground was broken for the Museum of the American Quilter's Society in August 1990, Bill and Meredith Schroeder had shared their dream, and I shared their excitement about the establishment of a new museum dedicated to today's quiltmaker.

As the museum's founding executive director, on loan from AQS part-time, I joined others on the outdoor stage for the grand opening on April 25, 1991, including Bill and Meredith Schroeder and their family, Paul Gresham (building architect), Craig Guess of Vanguard Contracting (building contractor), and Gerry Montgomery (city mayor and board member). And the grounds were filled with community members and visiting quilters, many of whom had also helped make this museum a reality — people like Paul D. Pilgrim and Gerald E. Roy, who had contributed much to the building's interior design and loaned wonderful antique quilts for an opening exhibit.

I have had the privilege of working with MAQS since that opening day, as a part-time executive director, then as curator of exhibits and director of programs in 1992 and 1993, and finally as full-time executive director from 1994 through 2001. It has been a pleasure to work closely with the founders, whose generosity and commitment to quality and service have been unending, and with a board of directors equally dedicated to the museum's mission.

Ruby Armstrong and Sherry Johnston, our initial gift shop manager and receptionist, remain a part of our team, but these ten years have also brought many new staff, all dedicated to our mission.

When we began the development of this book documenting our collection, it was envisioned as a way of helping visitors take the collection home with them, to share what they had experienced at our museum. As it developed, it became more than that. It became an introduction to quiltmaking, and ultimately it became a record of the people and programs connected with our activity these first ten years.

It is our hope that this publication will communicate how filled with activity these ten years have been, how exciting contemporary quiltmaking has been and continues to be, and how many people across the world it has taken to make MAQS the museum that it has become. Our thanks to all of you.

Victoria Faoro
Executive Director

IN HONOR OF

Victoria Faoro

CURATOR,
PRECEPTOR
& FRIEND

We'll miss you.
Bill & Meredith,
MAQS Staff,
AQS Staff

TOP: **Past and current members of the MAQS board of directors, gathered in the museum's conference room, which features three stained-glass windows based on quilt designs:** FRONT ROW (l to r) **Susan Talbot-Stanaway, Meredith Schroeder, Bettina Havig.** BACK ROW (l to r) **Lou Deluca, Linda Bond, Lynn Loyd, Susan Guess, Justin Hancock, Rick Loyd.**
PHOTO: CHARLES R. LYNCH

CLOSE UP_____

MAQS is governed by a board of directors that meets bi-monthly to oversee policies and planning for the museum. Direction is also provided by regional and national committees.

<u>2001 Directors</u>
Meredith Schroeder
David Bailey
Ann Denton
Justin Hancock
Lynn Loyd
Rick Loyd
Sylvia Mathis
Gerry Montgomery
Helen Thompson

<u>Past Directors</u>
Bill Schroeder
Dick Holland

<u>National Collections</u>
<u>Advisory Group</u>
Marty Bowne, ID
Libby Lehman, TX
Gerald E. Roy, NH

INTRODUCTION
The Museum

Since its opening in 1991, the Museum of the American Quilter's Society has introduced over 350,000 visitors to the extraordinary work of today's quiltmakers and those of the past through exhibits and programs. As is stated in the museum's mission statement, "MAQS is a non-profit institution established to educate the local, national, and international public about the art, history, and heritage of quiltmaking, including the diversity of quilts and their makers." MAQS accomplishes this mission through its professionally mounted exhibits, workshops, conferences, and publications, and through the development and exhibiting of its own collection and related archival materials.

Situated five miles off Interstate 24, fewer than 400 miles from Atlanta and Chicago, and fewer than 200 miles from St. Louis, Memphis, and Nashville, MAQS is easily visited by travelers. Those with a special interest in quilts often plan a north-south or east-west trip around an overnight visit to MAQS and the city of Paducah.

But many visitors are newly introduced to all that quilts and quiltmaking can be through their first visit to the museum, prompted by a highway sign, a friend's recommendation, or a planned group tour. Sometimes people have never realized that quilts could be more than bed covers, or quiltmakers could be of all ages and backgrounds.

At MAQS quilts are presented as visual art to be enjoyed for their excellence in design and craftsmanship. They are also presented as being connected with stories – the stories of their makers, their times, and their owners or caretakers. More than a celebration of quilts, MAQS is a celebration of quiltmakers, and exhibits often explore the way that quilts relate to their makers' lives.

Quilts are very special objects for many people. Perhaps it's because most of us have strong memories of what it is to touch a well-used quilt, to wrap up in it or sleep under it. Most of us have quilts in our families, and often even know someone who quilts. We are likely to have received a quilt as a gift. All of these connections affect the way we feel when we view a quilt on display. Often we are especially comfortable with quilts, we feel connected with them, and we want to know more about their stories.

The Museum of the American Quilter's Society feels privileged to be able to collect and display such important objects, and be able to preserve and share their stories.

OPPOSITE, CENTER: **Since the museum's opening, free guided tours have been provided for young people. Here students and their chaperones learn about antique quilts in an exhibit at MAQS coordinated by the New Jersey Quilt Project. Thousands of young people have been introduced to quiltmaking through school trips to view the exhibits at MAQS.**

OPPOSITE, BOTTOM: **Students often complete activities connected with quilts at MAQS. These students are learning how quilting is completed on a quilting frame, and also completing a school assignment connected with their viewing of the Patchworks of Remembrance and Hope quilts in progress in the lobby. See page 149 for more about that special project.**

ABOVE: **Museum of the American Quilter's Society.**

RIGHT: **THE MAP MAKERS**, 56" x 65½", is the Best in Contest winner of the Lewis and Clark Expedition Contest, 2003 AQS Quilt Exposition. Cassandra Williams, Grants Pass, OR, used a number of techniques to create this historical representation of the famed expedition.

RIGHT: **FLOATING**, 65" x 42" x4", is a solid wood sculpture by Fraser Smith, Tampa, FL. Appearing to be softly draped over a rope, the folds of Fraser's hanging quilt fool the eye. Tiny indentations mimic quilting stitches, but at more than 80 pounds this carved solid wood sculpture is anything but wrap-around cuddly.

THE FOUNDERS COLLECTION
Quilts

At the heart of any museum's activities are the important objects it was founded to collect, preserve, and share with the public.

The Museum of the American Quilter's Society (MAQS) was founded by Bill and Meredith Schroeder in 1991 to "honor today's quilter," and the quilt collection they began, the MAQS Founders Collection. It has become an ever-developing documentation of the quiltmaking revival that has flourished in the 1980s, 1990s, and is sure to continue as the new century unfolds.

The core of this collection includes quilts donated by the Schroeders and the AQS Quilt Show & Contest purchase award winners donated through the American Quilter's Society. Also included are a number of other donations and purchases.

MAQS is proud of this collection's comprehensive documentation of today's quiltmaking and the wide range of quilts and quiltmakers that it includes.

TOP: **Collection quilts first on display in April 1991. Gallery A was designed specifically to feature quilts from the museum's collection. Also visible in this photo are several quilts in The Color Orange exhibit and a quilt in the Quilts by AQS Authors exhibit.**
PHOTO: RICHARD WALKER

BOTTOM: **Collection quilts on display in Gallery A during fall 2000.**
PHOTO: CHARLES R. LYNCH

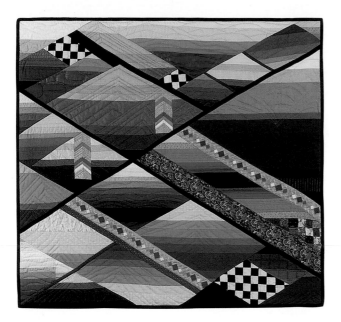

Connected
WITH PEOPLE
& PLACES

Quilts are often strongly connected with the people, places, and events in the lives of their makers. Sometimes a quilt is directly inspired by its maker's life; other times it becomes connected and influenced during the process. The making of a quilt, from idea, to design, to construction, often involves extended periods of time; it can span a major period in a person's life and become inextricably associated with their life experiences.

TOP: **Taos Tapestry,**
37" x 40", Laverne Mathews,
Orange, TX, 1986. Cottons and
cotton blends; machine pieced
and hand quilted.
MAQS 1997.06.81

BOTTOM: **Three for the Crown,**
54" x 54", Charlotte Warr Andersen,
Salt Lake City, UT, 1987. Silks;
hand pieced and hand quilted.
MAQS 1997.06.83

OPPOSITE, TOP: **Air Show,** 81" x 81",
Jonathan Shannon, Phoenix, AZ,
1992. Cottons; machine pieced,
hand appliquéd, couched cording,
and hand quilted.
MAQS 1996.01.01

OPPOSITE, BOTTOM: **Desert Dusk,**
53" x 43", Marguerite Ann Malwitz,
Brookfield, CT, 1988. Cottons,
blends, silks, and satins;
tie-dyed, machine and
hand pieced, hand quilted.
MAQS 1997.07.06

CLOSE UP

AIR SHOW was inspired by Jonathan Shannon's love of early airplanes – their design, their movement, their romantic images. He set out to create in fabric a sense of air and the weight of air that holds up airplanes. The back of his quilt features an additional airplane.

THREE FOR THE CROWN grew out of Charlotte Warr Andersen's love of horses and watching horse races. She has been drawing horses since she was a small child, influenced by her father, a saddlemaker. With its 2,425 pieces, this quilt depicts the tracks for the three races that comprise the Triple Crown: the Kentucky Derby, the Preakness, and the Belmont. In addition, the traditional blocks selected have names that relate to her overall theme.

TAOS TAPESTRY and DESERT DUSK were both inspired by landscapes, the latter by a visit to Desert Botanical Gardens in Phoenix, Arizona.

Nature can inspire a quiltmaker to make a traditional MAPLE LEAF quilt in colors remembered from a Vermont fall. A floral centerpiece at a reception can inspire a quiltmaker to create an original block and a quilt: CELEBRATION OF AUTUMN. Its centerpiece chrysanthemums and plumes of dyed pampas grass capture the energy of the event. A pattern like GRAND-MOTHER'S ENGAGEMENT RING can be made to celebrate an engagement (another quilt was later given to Arlene Statz's daughter). A quilt can connect people in its making: SOPHISTICATION was made by Margaret Rudd, working with a middle school student in a project designed to bring together "the vision of youth and the skill of maturity."

Close Up_____

Ruth B. McDowell is known for her quilts that adapt nature to the quilting medium. She explains, "I try to distill the essence of the subject, leaving out much more than I put in to uncover the spirit." Her quilt NA PALI was the result of her first visit to the Na Pali coast of Kauai, Hawaii, in 1999. The valley depicted is the Kalalau Valley, a site of historic and mythological significance that is almost inaccessible even today. This remarkable landscape is very different from the time-worn, glacier-smoothed rocks of New England.

Everyday scenes can inspire. On visits to her daughter, Jane Blair became fascinated with a nearby field of sunflowers and decided to capture in a quilt these late fall RAGGEDY SUN WORSHIPPERS. One of the childhood pastimes of Adabelle Dremann (1910 – 1992) was sketching pictures. Twenty-five years later she turned a sketch of the CORN CRIB on her farm into a quilt. In 1991, Adabelle commented, "The years grow shorter now, but are full of many rewarding memories." Lucretia Romey's CITYSCAPE was inspired by sketches she had done of the Toronto skyline, from the seventh floor of the Westbury Hotel. All of her wall quilts "are a result of drawings done in the yard or while traveling." Signatures also connect quilts with people and times. GALAXY OF QUILTERS includes 64 signature blocks honoring those who significantly contributed to the quilt world during the 1980s, as well as a block honoring "the hundreds of fine quilters who have not signed in."

TOP: **Corn Crib,** 42" x 47", Adabelle Dremann, Princeton, IL, 1989. Cottons; machine pieced, hand appliquéd, hand embroidered, and hand quilted with trapunto. MAQS 1997.06.13

BOTTOM: **Raggedy Sun Worshippers,** 48" x 64", Jane Blair Wyomissing, PA, 1996. Cottons, cotton/polyesters; hand appliquéd, hand and machine pieced, and hand quilted. MAQS 1996.04.01

OPPOSITE, TOP: **Garden Maze,** 82" x 82", Irma Gail Hatcher, Conway, AR, 1998. Cottons; machine pieced, hand appliquéd, and hand quilted with trapunto. MAQS 2000.02.01

OPPOSITE, BOTTOM LEFT: **Galaxy of Quilters,** 87" x 107", Lois K. Ide, Bucyrus, OH, 1983. Cottons and cotton blends; hand appliquéd, hand embroidered, machine pieced, and hand quilted. MAQS 1997.06.25

OPPOSITE, BOTTOM RIGHT: **Cityscape,** 50" x 64", Lucretia Romey, East Orleans, MA, 1984. Cottons, cottons blends, and metallic fabrics; hand pieced and hand quilted. MAQS 1997.06.10

CLOSE UP_____

GARDEN MAZE was intended for Irma Gail Hatcher's daughter, Gailyn. It was meant to replace the first quilt Irma Gail had made for her, CONWAY ALBUM (I'M NOT FROM BALTIMORE), which had become a part of the MAQS collection! Many of the flowers in this quilt's blocks represent places where Irma Gail and her family have lived: sunflowers for Kansas, primroses for Missouri, cherries for Michigan, pansies for Arkansas, and trumpet flowers for her grandmother's home in Texas. The balls atop the fence around the garden maze were inspired by cement balls on some fences in Conway, Arkansas.

TOP: **Trees: Summer/Winter**
41" x 51", Chris Wolf Edmonds,
Lawrence, KS, 2000. Cotton, water-
based pigments; hand painted and
printed, machine pieced,
and machine quilted.
MAQS 2001.03.01

BOTTOM: **Listen to Your Mother**
43" x 43", Jean Ray Laury,
Clovis, CA, 1997. Cottons; hand
screen printed and machine quilted.
MAQS 2001.04.01

OPPOSITE, TOP: **The Progressive
Pictorial Quilt,** 44" x 44", artists in
America's Pictorial Quilts, coordi-
nated by Caron L. Mosey, 1986.
Cottons and cotton blends;
hand appliquéd, hand
embroidered, and hand quilted.
MAQS 1991.01.01

OPPOSITE, BOTTOM LEFT: **Freedom's
Cascade,** 44" x 66", Erika Carter,
Bellevue, WA, 1990.
Cottons; machine pieced,
hand appliquéd, and hand quilted.
MAQS 1997.06.24

OPPOSITE, BOTTOM RIGHT: **Boat in a
Bottle Sampler,** 80" x 92",
Lyn Peare Sandberg, Capitola, CA,
1988. Cottons; machine pieced
and hand quilted.
MAQS 1992.09.01

CLOSE UP_____

TREES: SUMMER/WINTER
is part of a series of portraits Chris Wolf Edmonds
has completed chronicling
sycamore and aspen trees.
She comments: "The
primary inspiration for my
work is life in all its forms.
As an artist and amateur
naturalist, I collect the
colors and patterns of the
world around me and
attempt to preserve them
in my hand-painted and
printed fabrics. I spend
part of every day outdoors
observing life in nature."

Everything from personal memories to internationally significant events can be found connected with quilts. In BOAT IN A BOTTLE SAMPLER Lyn Peare Sandberg says each bottle "contains a particular moment in a decade of sailing on the Monterey Bay." Jean Ray Laury, who has long provided commentary on the human experience through her often humorous quilts, captures life beautifully in LISTEN TO YOUR MOTHER.

Caron L. Mosey organized THE PROGRESSIVE PICTORI-AL QUILT in conjunction with the publication of her pictorial appliqué book, inviting artists featured in the book to participate. Erika Carter's quilt FREEDOM'S CASCADE was inspired by dramatic changes that occurred in East Germany with the breaking up of the Berlin Wall. She comments: "The gray, black, and white background symbolizes life under communist rule, a presence which greatly impacts the developing democracy represented by the confetti-like flowers."

TOP: **Dawn Splendor,** 94" x 94",
Nancy Ann Sobel,
Brooktondale, NY, 1991. Cottons;
machine pieced, hand appliquéd,
and hand quilted.
MAQS 1996.01.08

BOTTOM: **When Grandmother's Lily
Garden Blooms,** 62" x 82",
Eileen Bahring Sullivan, Alpharetta,
GA, 1990. Cottons and blends;
machine pieced, hand
embroidered, and hand quilted.
MAQS 1997.06.91

Flowers – and insects – have inspired quiltmakers throughout the ages. Eileen Bahring Sullivan explains that WHEN GRANDMOTHER'S LILY GARDEN BLOOMS was conceived when "...with a piecer's eye, I began to dissect the flower, with its many variations in size and angles."

In DAWN SPLENDOR, Nancy Ann Sobel set out to capture the flowers and other creatures she encountered on pre-dawn walks with her son in rural New York State. The quilt includes everything from glorious peonies to the tiny ants always found on their buds, embroidered in place. Quilting designs feature further flora, and the ever-present robins. Two spider webs appear in glistening metallic embroidery, inhabited by embroidered spiders. An escaping appliqué butterfly symbolizes Sylvia Pickell's wish to escape from the restrictions of traditional quiltmaking in her quilt ESCAPE FROM CIRCLE CITY.

TOP: **Silversword – Degener's Dream,** 97" x 97", Louise Young, Tioga, PA, 1988. Cottons; hand appliquéd and hand quilted. MAQS 1992.06.01

BOTTOM: **Escape from Circle City,** 76" x 86", Sylvia Pickell, Sumter, SC, 1987. Cottons and polyblends; machine pieced, hand appliquéd, and hand quilted. MAQS 1997.06.19

Traditional blocks can become imbued with personal meaning, connecting with their makers' lives. Linda Karel Sage selected a traditional house pattern for BROWN COUNTY LOG CABINS, but her treatment was influenced by the area in which she lives, Brown County, Indiana, which is "heavily wooded, the hilly countryside dotted by little log cabins." Julee Prose made the traditional Barn Raising set for her Log Cabin blocks literally a COMMUNITY BARN RAISING, with appliquéd "Amish buggies winding through the countryside" in the borders. In OUTLOOKS Barbara Lydecker Crane turns traditional Attic Windows into a wall of stone with locked openings. In BEACH ROSES Joyce Murrin enjoys the way her original rose blocks disappear because of the fabric colors, which she suggests, allow the roses depicted "to look more like they do in nature."

TOP: **Outlooks** 60" x 54", Barbara Lydecker Crane, Lexington, MA, 1984. Cottons and cotton blends; hand pieced, machine pieced, hand quilted, and embellished with small objects. MAQS 1997.06.53

BOTTOM: **Pandas 'Round the World,** 75" x 99", Shirley P. Kelly, Colden, NY, 1993. Cottons; hand appliquéd, machine pieced, and machine quilted. MAQS 1997.07.14

OPPOSITE, TOP: **Beach Roses** 79" x 49", Joyce Murrin Orient, NY, 1986. Cottons and cotton blends, some hand dyed; machine pieced and hand quilted. MAQS 1997.06.05

OPPOSITE, BOTTOM LEFT: **Community Barn Raising** 78" x 102", Julee Prose, Ottumwa, IA, 1987. Cottons; hand appliquéd, machine pieced, and hand quilted. MAQS 1997.06.12

OPPOSITE, BOTTOM RIGHT: **Brown County Log Cabins** 87" x 93", Linda Karel Sage, Morgantown, IN, 1985. Cottons; machine pieced and hand quilted. MAQS 1997.06.08

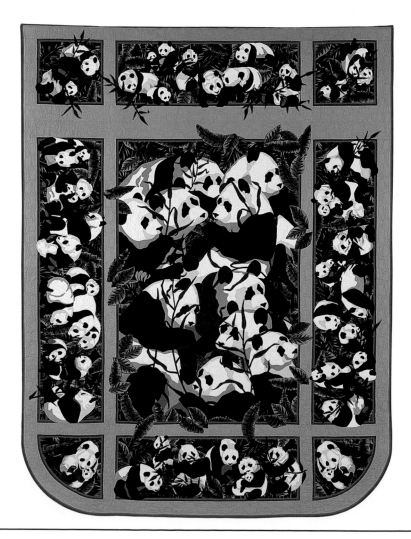

CLOSE UP_____

PANDAS 'ROUND THE WORLD was based on photos taken when Shirley P. Kelly took her children to the National Zoo to see Ling-Ling and Hsing-Hsing. The trip had inspired an obsession with pandas. Kelly comments: "At last count, fewer than 1,000 wild pandas are found in two small preserves where human encroachment still threatens what is left of their fragile environment." This quilt (front and back) features about 10% of the 1993 population.

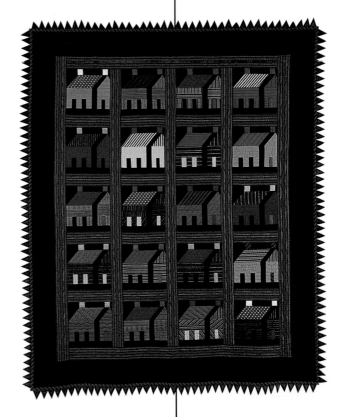

TOP: **Looking Back on Broken Promises,** 53" x 38", Dawn Amos, Rapid City, SD, 1989. Cottons, hand dyed; hand appliquéd and hand quilted. MAQS 1996.01.16

BOTTOM: **The Mountain and the Magic: Night Lights,** 65" x 65", Judi Warren Blaydon, Milford, MI, 1995. Lamé, rayon, American and Japanese cottons, antique kimono silk; machine pieced, hand quilted, hand appliquéd, and hand beaded. MAQS 2001.02.01

OPPOSITE, TOP LEFT: **Mount St. Helens, Did You Tremble?** 79" x 95", Joyce B. Peaden, Prosser, WA, 1990. Cottons; hand appliquéd, machine pieced, Seminole pieced, and hand quilted. MAQS 1991.02.01

OPPOSITE, TOP RIGHT: **Ice Fantasia** 74" x 87", Elsie Vredenburg, Tustin, MI, 1989. Cottons; machine pieced and hand quilted. MAQS 1992.10.01

OPPOSITE, BOTTOM: **Here Between,** 40.5" x 40.5", Marilyn Henrion, New York, NY, 1992. Cottons; machine pieced and hand quilted. MAQS 1997.07.12

CLOSE UP_____

Judi Warren Blaydon remembers: "Our dinner cruise boat carrying one cook, one waiter, and 27 quiltmakers floated on Tokyo Bay in the darkness. This boat and others were lit by rows of paper lanterns; the lights of the city glimmered in the distance; all around us were glowing reflections of light and color dancing on the black water."

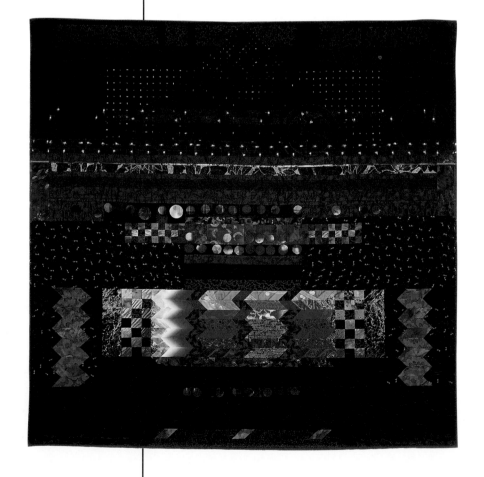

Events and situations inspire quilts. The 1988 Winter Olympics figure skating competition and a quilt show's Fan theme inspired ICE FANTASIA with its border of watching fans. Dawn Amos tried to put "the viewer in the Native American's place" in her quilt LOOK-ING BACK ON BROKEN PROMISES. She comments: "It would be nice to think that I could make some sort of impression on people through my quilts." On May 25, 1980, the day of the secondary eruption of Mount St. Helens, a poem flew into the mind of Joyce B. Peaden, and her quilt MOUNT ST. HELENS, DID YOU TREMBLE? followed shortly after.

The title for Marilyn Henrion's quilt HERE BETWEEN was drawn from a T.S. Eliot poem: "Here between the hither and farther shore, / While time is withdrawn, consider the future / And the past with an equal mind." This quilt was made as a fund-raiser for the American Quilt Study Group, to commemorate the bridge that the quilt medium forms between past, present, and future.

Caryl Bryer Fallert made RED POPPIES as a commissioned piece for a couple living in an old farm house full of antiques. When this variation on the Kaleidoscope pattern was completed, Fallert thought it was too contemporary for the house and kept it, making a new quilt for her clients. Donna Duchesne Garofalo's quilt, SERENITY II: LIFE IN MY POND, was made purely for her own enjoyment, depicting her "love and respect for God's creation and its beauty."

VOICE OF FREEDOM, based on the Lincoln Memorial, was one of many quilts designed for a contest celebrating the birthday of the Statue of Liberty. Yvonne Porcella responded to the 1995 bombing of the federal building in Oklahoma City with ON WEDNESDAY MORNING, a quilt that reflects both the love and loss associated with the event. The quilt honors in particular the 19 children for whom there will be no more "Sesame Street®," Kermit the Frog, or Mr. Potato Head®. The outpouring of love shown to the victims is reflected in the spray of hearts.

CLOSE UP_____

MOUNT PLEASANT MINERS is a tribute to Nancy S. Brown's great-grandfather, who worked at the Mount Pleasant Mine in Grizzly Flats, California, for 17 years as a blacksmith and later as a superintendent. The design was based on an 1870's photo of 36 miners, including her great-grandfather. She selected 15 of the miners and rearranged them. Nancy also "buried" a few flakes of gold under a rock next to her great-grandfather's right elbow. She comments: "In proportion to the rest of the scene it would be several nuggets."

OPPOSITE, TOP: **Serenity II: Life in My Pond,** 42" x 57", Donna Duchesne Garofalo, North Windham, CT, 1985. Cottons, cotton blends; machine pieced, hand quilted, and hand appliquéd. MAQS 1997.06.69

OPPOSITE, BOTTOM: **Mount Pleasant Miners,** 48" x 55", Nancy S. Brown, Oakland, CA 1993. Cottons, hand dyed and painted; hand appliquéd, machine pieced, and hand quilted. MAQS 1996.01.20

TOP LEFT: **Voice of Freedom** 66" x 65", Barbara Temple, Mesa, AZ, 1987. Cottons; hand appliquéd and hand quilted. MAQS 1997.06.90

TOP RIGHT: **Red Poppies,** 72" x 90", Caryl Bryer Fallert, Oswego, IL, 1983. Cottons; machine pieced and hand quilted. MAQS 1997.06.62

RIGHT: **On Wednesday Morning,** 50" x 70", Yvonne Porcella, Modesto, CA, 1995. Cottons; machine pieced and hand quilted MAQS 2001.10.01

APPLIQUÉ *Quilts*

Appliqué, the technique of cutting shapes from fabrics and applying them to a background by hand or by machine, is a very versatile technique for quiltmaking, and one commonly used by quiltmakers both in the past and today. Traditionally, appliqué was often used to produce floral or other pictorial designs, sometimes with embroidery and other techniques incorporated to add details.

In traditional appliqué quilts there was often much contrast between the background fabric and the appliquéd shapes, as with the red and green shapes on white in CHERRY ROSE, the appliquéd shapes filling the center of MOMMA'S GARDEN, and even the designs in Linda Goodmon Emery's ROSEMALING INSPIRATION. The appliqué in SPRING WINDS was unusual for the mid 1980s in that it was done on a print fabric rather than a solid. Faye Anderson comments: "Since making this quilt I have consciously tried to use prints rather than solids, because it is pattern that most obviously distinguishes works in fabric from those in other mediums, such as paint.''

TOP: **Move Over Matisse I**
36" x 70", Virginia Avery
Port Chester, NY, 1980.
Cottons; hand appliquéd
and hand quilted.
MAQS 2001.01.01

BOTTOM: **Cherry Rose**
95" x 94", Margie T. Karavitis,
Spokane, WA, 1989. Cottons;
hand appliquéd, hand and
machine pieced, and hand quilted.
MAQS 1992.13.01

OPPOSITE, TOP: **Spring Winds**
76" x 87", Faye Anderson,
Boulder, CO, 1985.
Cottons; hand appliquéd
and hand quilted.
MAQS 1996.01.24

OPPOSITE, BOTTOM LEFT: **Momma's Garden,** 88" x 91", Anne J.
Oliver, Alexandria, VA, 1992.
Cottons; hand appliquéd
and hand quilted.
MAQS 1996.01.19

OPPOSITE, BOTTOM RIGHT: **Rosemaling Inspiration,** 81" x 95"
Linda Goodmon Emery,
Derby, KS, 1986. Cottons and
flexible ribbon floss embellishment;
hand appliquéd and hand quilted.
MAQS 1997.06.65

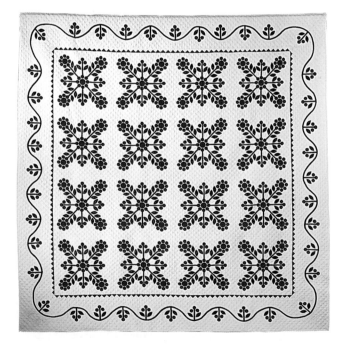

CLOSE UP_____

Appliqué can also be used for abstract shapes against a colored background, as in Virginia Avery's bold MOVE OVER MATISSE I, a quilt based on Matisse's cut-paper art. Avery feels like this piece represents well her continued use of abstract shapes of vivid colors and her "free-wheeling" approach to appliqué. She enjoys working with bright jewel tones and black, which "adds depth to everything."

Appliqué can be used in combination with pieced designs, as in CHIPS AND WHETSTONES, where appliquéd shapes appear between pieced blocks and throughout the border, with its elaborate twists.

Appliqué can be used to create separate quilt blocks that can then be joined to create a quilt, as in CROWN OF CERISE. Or a large center design can be appliquéd, as in ORIENTAL FANTASY, with borders then added to complete the overall quilt shape. In this case, the design in the border areas features appliqué as well, along with quilting.

In some cases, the entire surface of a quilt can become a large canvas for appliqué, as in TWELVE DAYS OF CHRISTMAS, which features elements of the song in detail.

TOP: **Oriental Fantasy,** 82" x 98", Katherine Inman, Athens, OH, 1985. Cottons; hand appliquéd, hand embroidered, and hand quilted. MAQS 1996.01.22

BOTTOM: **Chips and Whetstones,** 80" x 89.5", Martha B. Skelton, Vicksburg, MS, 1987. Cottons; hand and machine pieced, hand appliquéd, and hand quilted. MAQS 1992.02.01

OPPOSITE, TOP: **Twelve Days of Christmas,** 102" x 108", B.J. Elvgren, Chesapeake, VA, 1983. Cottons, velvets, and silks; hand appliquéd, hand quilted with trapunto, and hand embroidered. MAQS 1997.06.88

OPPOSITE, BOTTOM: **Crown of Cerise,** 94" x 94", Rose Sanders, Harahan, LA, 1986. Cottons; hand appliquéd and hand quilted with trapunto. MAQS 1997.07.05

CLOSE UP_____

B. J. Elvgren designed THE TWELVE DAYS OF CHRISTMAS to "capture the spirit of Christmas and comment that the gift of the Christ-child should be central to that spirit." The quilt became a challenge to use a single design to contain the twelve groups featured in the song: 1 partridge, 2 turtle doves, 3 French hens, 4 calling birds, 5 golden rings, 6 geese a-laying, 7 swans a-swimming, 8 maids a-milking, 9 ladies dancing, 10 lords a-leaping, 11 pipers piping, and 12 drummers drumming.

Elvgren adds, "The Madonna and Christ-child were added as a comment on the foundation of gift-giving at Christmas." Note that even the outer edges of the shape are pictorial, becoming the stable setting for the Madonna and Christ-child.

The Baltimore Album quilt is a style that originally gained popularity in the mid 1800s, and has enjoyed renewed interest in the 1980s and 1990s. BALTIMORE REMEMBERED is based on appliqué patterns traditionally used in these quilts, featuring different designs in their pictorial blocks, often made by different quiltmakers. Aileen Stannis based many of her blocks on Elly Sienkiewicz's patterns.

Floral appliqué is combined with pieced elements in OUR SECRET GARDEN, which is named after *The Secret Garden,* Donna Fite McConnell's favorite childhood book, and in MORNING GLORY, which includes a floral wreath center based on a Nancy Pearson pattern. Beginning with the pieced Tumbling Block body, in PHOENIX RISING, Nancy Clark created in appliqué that mythical creature with the same name as her city of residence.

TOP: **Our Secret Garden,** 87" x 87", Donna Fite McConnell and Patricia Eaton, Searcy, AR, 1990. Cottons; machine pieced, hand appliquéd, and hand quilted. MAQS 1997.06.52

BOTTOM: **Baltimore Remembered,** 83" x 103", Aileen Stannis, Berkley, MI, 1996. Cottons; hand appliquéd, hand pieced, and hand quilted. MAQS 1996.03.01

OPPOSITE, TOP: **Vintage Rose Garden,** 94" x 94.5", Judith Thompson, Wenonah, NJ, 1996. Cottons, new and vintage; hand appliquéd, hand pieced, and hand quilted. MAQS 1997.04.01

OPPOSITE, BOTTOM LEFT: **Morning Glory,** 80" x 100", Mary Chartier, New London, CT, 1986. Cottons; hand appliquéd, hand and machine pieced, and hand quilted. MAQS 1992.17.01

OPPOSITE, BOTTOM RIGHT: **Phoenix Rising,** 95.5" x 80", Nancy Clark, Phoenix, AZ, 1987. Cottons; machine pieced, hand appliquéd, hand painted, and hand quilted. MAQS 1997.06.56

CLOSE UP_____

Judith Thompson's VIN-
TAGE ROSE GARDEN
combines new and old
fabrics in an album or
sampler of floral blocks.
In some cases Thompson
has used a vintage fabric
and a modern-day
reproduction of that same
fabric. Today's fabric man-
ufacturers have released a
number of lines of fabrics
based on antique fabrics.
The fabrics in Thompson's
quilt are endlessly varied,
with brightly colored
contemporary plaids
appearing in sashing
strips and corner squares,
often intentionally mis-
matched to add life and
movement.

TOP: **President's Wreath Variation,** 72" x 96" (shown sideways), Doris Amiss Rabey, Hyattsville, MD, 1986. Cottons and cotton/polyesters; hand appliquéd, machine pieced, and hand quilted. MAQS 1997.06.58

BOTTOM: **Javanese Jungle,** 75" x 94", Audree L. Sells, Chaska, MN, 1987. Cottons; hand pieced, hand appliquéd, hand embroidered and beaded, and hand quilted. MAQS 1992.16.01

OPPOSITE, TOP: **Autumn Radiance,** 81" x 93", Sharon Rauba, Riverside, IL, 1986. Cottons and cotton blends; hand appliquéd, machine pieced, and hand quilted. MAQS 1996.01.03

OPPOSITE, BOTTOM LEFT: **Tulips in a Basket,** 87" x 108", Marjorie D. Townsend, Parsons, TN, 1984. Cottons; hand appliquéd and hand quilted. MAQS 1997.06.87

OPPOSITE, BOTTOM RIGHT: **Country School,** 73" x 92", Adabelle Dremann, Princeton, IL, 1988. Cottons; machine pieced, hand appliquéd, and hand quilted. MAQS 1992.01.01

CLOSE UP_____

JAVANESE JUNGLE was inspired by an original batik by Emilie Von Kerckhoff, a Dutch artist known for her paintings and batiks. It was featured on the November 1933 cover of *Needlecraft: The Home Arts Magazine.* In Sells' quilt, note the three-dimensional elephant's ear, created by appliquéing to the quilt a two-sided, padded ear.

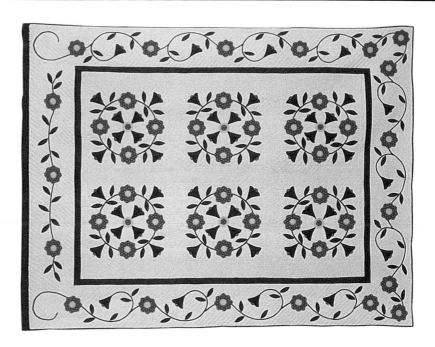

As with other types of quilts, appliqué designs are inspired by a wide range of situations. For Marjorie D. Townsend, quilting is a family tradition. She learned the fundamentals early in life and later began to think of quilting as an art form, in the early 1980s. TULIPS IN A BASKET is adapted from a pattern in the *Better Homes and Gardens Treasury of Needlecrafts.*

Love of nature inspired Sharon Rauba's AQS Best of Show quilt AUTUMN RADIANCE, with its many appliquéd leaves. COUNTRY SCHOOL was based on the late Adabelle Dremann's fond memories of a one-room country school, like the one in which her children started their education in Bureau Country, Illinois.

Doris Amis Rabey explains that PRESIDENT'S WREATH VARIATION did not start out as a variation. She explains: "After cutting, I discovered the pattern was mismarked so I had to make radical changes." The quiltmaking process often involves creative responses to unexpected problems with a pattern, insufficient amounts of fabric, or other "challenges." It is often the need to problem solve or improvise that stimulates personalization of a design.

Love of flowers and love of hand appliqué often come together to make beautiful quilt designs. NATURE'S WALK is made in the traditional style of the striking center-interest floral quilts designed in the 1920s and 1930s. ORCHARD BEAUTY, inspired by spring blossoms, features a large rectangular center panel with soft floral appliqué, resembling a pictorial scene.

Irma Gail Hatcher's CONWAY ALBUM (I'M NOT FROM BALTIMORE) is filled with floral appliqué blocks, many of which include three-dimensional areas. This Baltimore Album-style quilt center is surrounded by a swag border with additional floral designs. WILD ROSE works its magic with a more stylized floral pattern called Whig Rose. Note the secondary pattern of floral wreaths formed between the Whig Rose blocks.

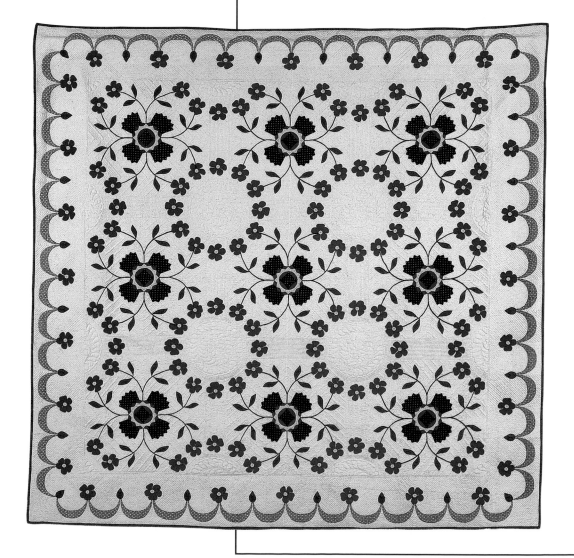

OPPOSITE, TOP: **Nature's Walk,**
99" x 103", Hazel B. Reed Ferrell,
Middlebourne, WV, 1983.
Cotton blends; hand appliquéd
and hand quilted.
MAQS 1997.06.41

OPPOSITE, BOTTOM: **Wild Rose,**
90" x 90", Fay Pritts,
Mt. Pleasant, PA, 1993. Cottons;
hand appliquéd and hand quilted.
MAQS 1996.01.30

TOP: **Conway Album (I'm Not from
Baltimore),** 86" x 89",
Irma Gail Hatcher, Conway, AR,
1992. Cottons; hand appliquéd
and hand quilted.
MAQS 1996.01.06

BOTTOM: **Orchard Beauty,**
88" x 105", Toni Kron,
Guntersville, AL, 1986. Dacron/
cotton blends; hand appliquéd
and hand quilted.
MAQS 1997.06.50

CLOSE UP_____

Three-dimensional
appliqué adds fascinating
texture to CONWAY
ALBUM (I'M NOT FROM
BALTIMORE). Circular
yellow flowers are created
using ruching, a technique
in which a strip of gath-
ered fabric is laid in
concentric circles to build
a raised flower center.
Also featured are folded
buds, stuffed berries, and
other dimensional accents.

TOP: **Descending Visions**, 46" x 62", Dawn Amos, Rapid City, SD, 1992. Hand-dyed cottons; hand appliquéd and hand quilted. MAQS 1996.01.09

BOTTOM: **Basket of Flowers**, 72" x 82", Marzenna J. Krol, Carmel Valley, CA, 1982. Cottons/ polyesters; hand appliquéd and hand quilted. MAQS 1997.06.03

OPPOSITE, TOP: **Poppies and Other California Beauties**, 88" x 112", Canyon Quilters of San Diego, San Diego, CA, 1990. Cottons; hand appliquéd, hand embroidered, and hand quilted. MAQS 1992.20.01

OPPOSITE, BOTTOM LEFT: **Feathered Friends**, 63" x 91", Carolyn and Wilma Johnson, Symsonia, KY, 1984. Cottons; hand appliquéd and hand quilted. MAQS 1997.06.20

OPPOSITE, BOTTOM RIGHT: **Buffalo Magic**, 75" x 90", Barbara Pettinga Moore, Shelburne, VT, 1984. Cotton broadcloth, suede cloth; hand appliquéd and hand quilted. MAQS 1997.06.09

Appliqué frequently is used when quiltmakers want to capture an object from life quite realistically. FEATHERED FRIENDS caught the eye of MAQS's co-founder Bill Schroeder because of the realistic detail in the different species featured in appliqué. In BUFFALO MAGIC appliqué depicts museum artifacts Barbara Pettinga Moore had sketched. She visited museums en route to her summer employment as a park ranger in Badlands National Park in South Dakota, gathering images for this quilt, her first appliqué quilt. Suede, which does not have raw edges that need to be turned, was used for the images, allowing for finer details and more narrow shapes to be appliquéd.

Marzenna J. Krol speaks of arranging her fabric appliqué pieces in BASKET OF FLOWERS as though she were arranging dried flowers. Dawn Amos used appliqué and reverse appliqué, in which a shape is cut out of the appliqué piece and the edges turned under to expose a fabric beneath, to create the images in DESCENDING VISIONS.

CLOSE UP_____

The quilt POPPIES AND OTHER CALIFORNIA BEAUTIES was inspired by the Baltimore Album tradition and California's abundant flora. It was designed by Donalene Rasmussen as an opportunity quilt for Canyon Quilters of San Diego. Members who wished to participate selected a block to complete using Rasmussen's fabrics and design. A number of members also assisted with the quilting. This quilt, nine months in the making, generated donations, and its winner then donated the quilt to MAQS. Quilts have traditionally been used to raise funds for groups and projects.

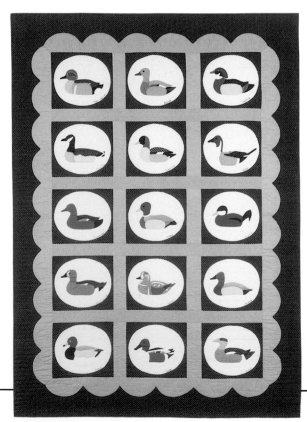

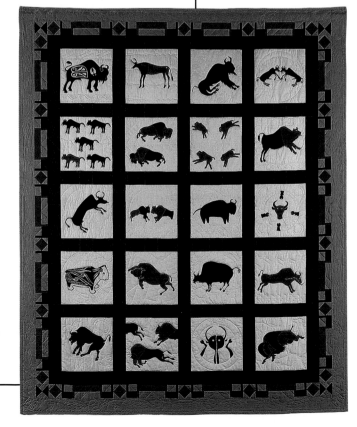

Appliqué quilts are sometimes inspired by contests. Faye Anderson's GARDEN PARTY was made to enter in *Quilter's Newsletter Magazine's* 200th issue contest. LANCASTER COUNTY ROSE was made by Irene Goodrich for a National Quilting Association contest. Numbered patterns were sold as a fund-raiser, and the contest quilts were hung at the 11th NQA Show in July 1980.

The inspiration for an appliqué quilt may be the splashy color of a seasonal bloom, as in BLAZING SPLENDOR by Marlene Brown Woodfield; traditional flowers patterns like those in Doris Amiss Rabey's FEATHERED STAR BOUQUET; or May flowers like those that inspired identical twin sisters Jean Evans and Joyce Murrin to create MAY SHADOWS.

TOP: **May Shadows,** 60" x 60", Jean M. Evans, Medina, OH, and Joyce Murrin, Orient, NY, 1985. Cottons, cotton blends; hand appliquéd and hand quilted. MAQS 1997.06.39

BOTTOM: **Garden Party,** 83" x 98.5", Faye Anderson, Boulder, CO, 1987. Cottons; machine pieced, hand appliquéd, hand embroidered, and hand quilted. MAQS 1992.05.01

OPPOSITE, TOP: **Feathered Star Bouquet,** 77" x 77", Doris Amiss Rabey, Hyattsville, MD, 1987. Cottons; hand quilted and appliquéd. MAQS 1992.03.01

OPPOSITE, BOTTOM LEFT: **Lancaster County Rose,** 90" x 110", Irene Goodrich, Columbus, OH, 1980. Cottons and cotton blends; hand pieced and hand quilted. MAQS 1997.06.31

OPPOSITE, BOTTOM RIGHT: **Blazing Splendor,** 38" x 60", Marlene Brown Woodfield, LaPorte, IN, 1986. Cotton blends; hand appliquéd, hand embroidered, and hand quilted. MAQS 1997.06.07

CLOSE UP_____

Faye Anderson explains that the most challenging aspect of designing her appliqué quilt GARDEN PARTY was placing the animals in "a harmonious way so that they would all be looking in the direction of the serpent. Twining the snake on the vine in a realistic manner also took hours of playing with a flexible curve and a piece of cording."

The flower cluster designs in Ethel Hickman's ANN ORR'S "YE OLD SAMPLER" are adaptations of floral patterns created by Tennessee quilt pattern designer Ann Orr for a quilt she called "Ye Olde Sampler." Hickman developed quilting designs to add to the graceful lines of the appliqué motifs.

Frances Stone's quilt-in-progress, "My Blue Shadow," was re-named PEACE AND LOVE by her husband because the rose suggested to him the Peace rose he had planted in their garden as a gift for her shortly after their marriage.

Barbara Brunner loves roses and tulips but doesn't have a flower garden – all her flowers are found on quilts like ROSES FOR A JUNE BRIDE. The shapes in an Oriental rug Jean K. Mathews purchased in Greece in 1985 inspired the appliqué shapes in her quilt, PERSIAN PARADISE.

CLOSE UP_____

Suzanne Marshall found the Art Nouveau designs in TOUJOURS NOUVEAU some of the most difficult appliqué designs she had ever done. The order in which the seemingly interwoven curving ribbons were to be stitched was determined as the sewing evolved. Soft colors were used for the gentle flow of the design elements.

OPPOSITE, TOP LEFT: **Persian Paradise,** 59" x 72.5", Jean K. Mathews, Marco Island, FL, 1986. Cottons and polyester/cotton chintz; hand appliquéd, reverse appliquéd, and hand quilted.
MAQS 1997.06.55

OPPOSITE, TOP RIGHT: **Roses for a June Bride,** 84" x 109", Barbara Brunner, Schofield, WI, 1986. Cottons; hand appliquéd and hand quilted.
MAQS 1997.06.67

OPPOSITE, BOTTOM: **Ann Orr's "Ye Olde Sampler,"** 80" x 100", Ethel Hickman, Camden, AR, 1985. Poly/cotton blends, cottons; hand appliquéd, hand quilted with corded edge.
MAQS 1997.06.02

TOP: **Peace and Love,** 96" x 92", Frances Stone, Mayfield, KY, 1985. Cottons, lace, and ribbon; hand quilted with embroidery thread.
MAQS 1997.06.54

BOTTOM: **Toujours Nouveau,** 69" x 80", Suzanne Marshall, Clayton, MO, 1993. Cottons; hand appliquéd with embroidery and hand quilted.
MAQS 1996.01.27

PIECED
Quilts

Pieced quilts are a strong tradition. In pieced quilts, separate fabric pieces are seamed, or stitched together along their edges rather than being applied to a background. Frequently these quilts have a unit design called a block. Often square, this unit is repeated to create the overall design, as in SUNBURST QUILT and DREAMCATCHER. Other times this unit is repeated in only a portion of the quilt, as in LILIES IN AUTUMN, or a different design approach is taken as in SUBMERGENCE.

TOP LEFT: **Lilies of Autumn,** 70" x 74", Juanita Gibson Yeager, Louisville, KY, 1991. Cottons; hand pieced and hand quilted.
MAQS 1997.06.32

TOP RIGHT: **Sunburst Quilt,** 90" x 89", Debra Wagner, Cosmos, MN, 1994. Cottons; machine pieced and machine quilted with trapunto.
MAQS 1996.01.25

BOTTOM: **Submergence,** 71" x 53", Erika Carter, Bellevue, WA, 1989. Cottons; machine pieced, hand appliquéd, and hand quilted.
MAQS 1997.06.79

CLOSE UP_____

The MAQS collection celebrates both hand and machine pieced quilts, in all their diversity. Juanita Gibson Yeager pieced LILIES OF AUTUMN by hand. She comments: "I came to quiltmaking with no art training, only a desire and strong emotional commitment to create visual beauty with my hands from cloth." Becky Brown, like many quiltmakers, enjoys the "portability" of hand work. She cut the first pieces for her hand-pieced DREAMCATCHER "in preparation for a two-week vacation trip to Kansas."

Erika Carter creates the water surface in SUBMERGENCE working entirely by machine, and Debra Wagner has written books helping others achieve her extraordinary accuracy in pieced designs. SUNBURST QUILT was entirely machine pieced for the Vermont Quilt Festival, to be used as their raffle quilt. When the quilt won a Purchase Award, the Festival graciously allowed it to be donated to MAQS.

TOP: **Dreamcatcher,**
66" x 82", Becky Brown,
Richmond, VA, 1994.
Cottons; hand pieced,
hand appliquéd, and hand quilted.
MAQS 1997.07.08

BOTTOM: **Detail of Sunburst Quilt.**

CLOSE UP_____

Traditional pieced blocks often have fascinating stories concerning their origin, and frequently also have contemporary quiltmakers with whom their exceptional use is associated.

The Mariner's Compass design, explored in Judy Mathieson's NEW DIRECTIONS, is a traditional block pattern – a star design that radiates from a circle rather than a square. Usually it includes 16 or 32 points. The design relates to the symbols used on sixteenth-century sailing charts.

With its very elongated points and circular design, this pattern requires a great deal of accuracy in its piecing. Mathieson, who has been working with this design since 1979 and has written two books on the subject, is the contemporary quiltmaker most associated with this design. She has made many quilts using it and finds it still remains her favorite pattern. NEW DIRECTIONS includes a wide array of these pieced stars, all taken from her book *Mariner's Compass Quilts: New Directions.*

TOP: **New Directions,** *76" x 92",* Judy Mathieson, Sebastopol, CA, 1996. Cottons; machine pieced, hand appliquéd, and hand and machine quilted. MAQS 2001.07.01

Pieced designs can be based on traditional designs, commercial patterns, or original designs. Polly Sepulvado's GRANDMOTHER'S ENGAGEMENT RING, which involves both piecing and appliqué, was made using a Mountain Mist batting company pattern based on this traditional design. On page 16 is another quilt based on that same commercial pattern. Arleen Boyd's ROSES BY STARLIGHT was inspired by a rose print fabric, which she used with a traditional star block. Adrien Rothschild created her own pieced design for her tree quilt, and used such a wide array of colors that, as a former student of molecular biology, she decided she should call the quilt DESIGNER CHRISTMAS TREES, ascribing the unusual colors to genetic engineering.

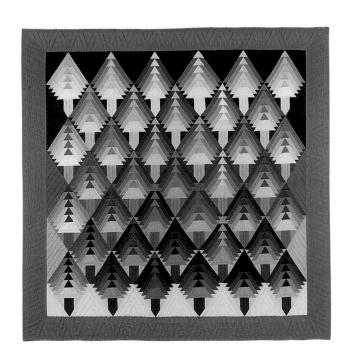

TOP LEFT: **Designer Christmas Trees,**
62" x 62", Adrien Rothschild,
Baltimore, MD, 1990. Hand-dyed
cottons; machine pieced
and hand quilted.
MAQS 1991.03.01

TOP RIGHT: **Roses by Starlight,** 89" x
100.5", Arleen Boyd, Rochester,
NY, 1985. Cottons; machine
pieced and hand quilted.
MAQS 1997.06.66

LEFT: **Grandmother's
Engagement Ring,**
76" x 94" (shown sideways),
Polly Sepulvado, M.D.,
Roseburg, OR, 1986.
Cottons; hand appliquéd, machine
pieced, and hand quilted.
MAQS 1997.06.27

P ieced designs are inspired by as varied a range of people, objects, and situations as are other designs. Fabrics and traditional designs sometimes come into play. Mary Kay Hitchner found a floral repeat stripe fabric she thought would be a challenge, and had just given a review of Marsha McCloskey's book *The Feathered Star*. Thus began Hitchner's quilt TULIPS AGLOW, with its Feathered Star pieced design at the center.

Libby Lehman found a pieced star design perfect to make her quilt STAR-CROSSED, celebrating her home state of Texas, the Lone Star State. It was technology that finally enabled Caryl Bryer Fallert to make BIRDS OF A DIFFERENT COLOR, a design idea she had had for some years. Using her computer, she could quickly re-size and re-position bird shapes to create this very complex pieced design.

TOP: **Tulips Aglow,** 54.5" x 54.5",
Mary Kay Hitchner,
Haverford, PA, 1989. Cottons;
machine pieced and hand quilted.
MAQS 1996.01.28

BOTTOM: **Birds of a Different Color,**
74" x 93", Caryl Bryer Fallert,
Oswego, IL, 1999.
Hand-dyed cottons; machine pieced
and machine quilted.
MAQS 2000.01.01

TOP: **Star-Crossed,** 70" x 70", Libby Lehman, Houston, TX, 1986. Cottons and cotton blends; machine pieced and hand quilted. MAQS 1997.06.76

BOTTOM: **A Li'l Bit Crazy Two,** 63" x 78", Anna Williams, Baton Rouge, LA, 1994; quilted by Mary Walker. Cottons; hand and machine pieced and hand quilted. MAQS 2001.09.01

Close Up_____

Anna Williams pieces her quilts using no patterns, improvising as she cuts and stitches. She usually has eight or nine quilts at a time, and works on a few blocks for two or three of them each evening. In her bedroom, which serves as a studio, she sits at her sewing machine with piles of fabric pieces to her side, cutting pieces freehand, judging size by eye. A LI'L BIT CRAZY TWO is constructed in the tradition of the string quilt, where narrow left-over scraps are stitched together and segments joined to make a quilt. Williams's lively arrangements bring much excitement to this tradition in scrap quiltmaking.

Williams freehand cutting strips for piecing.

TOP: **Star of Chamblie,** 67" x 67",
Marsha McCloskey, Seattle,
WA, 1986. Cottons; machine
pieced and hand quilted.
MAQS 2001.05.01

BOTTOM: **Sunset Kites,** 63" x 63",
Carol Ann Wadley, Hillsboro, OR,
1985. Cottons; machine pieced
and hand quilted.
MAQS 1997.06.80

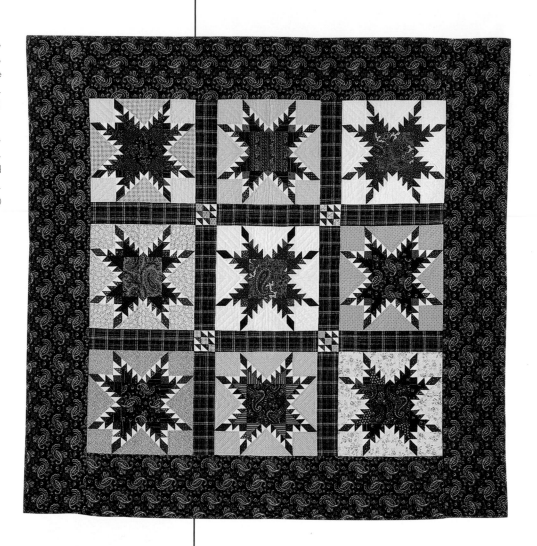

Traditional pieced patterns continue to inspire today's quiltmakers. Marsha McClosky is internationally renowned for her use of the traditional Feathered Star pattern in quilts such as STAR OF CHAMBLIE. Jane Hall is renowned for her work with pieced PINEAPPLE LOG CABIN design. The Log Cabin pattern, with its center square surrounded by "logs" or strips of fabric, dark on one side of the block and light on the other, has been a traditional favorite. Elsie Schlabach created AMISH MUTUAL AID using the Barn Raising set for her Log Cabin blocks. Martha B. Skelton, who makes quilts meant to be used, named hers for the pieced block she used: NEW YORK BEAUTY. Carol Ann Wadley made traditional bed quilts for many years, and then began to create original designs, such as SUNSET KITES.

CLOSE UP_____

Marsha McCloskey made STAR OF CHAMBLIE while researching her book *Feathered Star Quilts*. She drafted the pattern using Barbara Brackman's *Encyclopedia of Pieced Patterns*, a reference book with drawings of thousands of pieced patterns. McCloskey chose this pattern for her quilt because it provided a large center square for showcasing Paisley fabrics from her fabric collection.

TOP LEFT: **New York Beauty,** 77" x 90", Martha B. Skelton, Vicksburg, MS, 1986. Cottons; hand pieced, machine pieced, and hand quilted. MAQS 1997.06.44

TOP RIGHT: **Pineapple Log Cabin,** 50" x 68", Jane Hall, Raleigh, NC, 1985. Cottons; machine pieced and hand quilted. MAQS 1997.06.57

BOTTOM: **Amish Mutual Aid,** 75" x 83", Elsie Schlabach, Millersburg, OH, 1993. Cottons; machine pieced, hand pieced, and hand quilted. MAQS 1997.07.01

CLOSE UP_____

Working in creative ways with pieced designs was a specialty of Doreen Speckmann (1950 – 1999). She designed a series of combinations of geometric shapes, gave them descriptive names, and used them as building blocks for her quilts, generously sharing them with others in her workshops and her books. THE BLADE is composed of a Swamp Patch block laid over a Peaky and Spike With Ice Cream Cones block to make what she called a Wingra Star block.

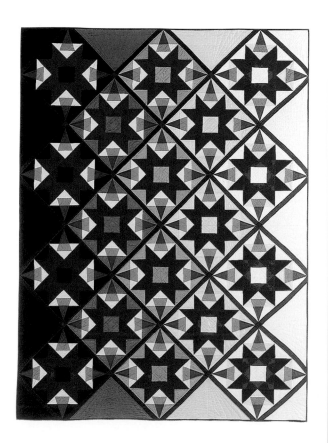

OPPOSITE, TOP: **Nothing Gold Can Stay,** 71" x 57", Marion Huyck, Chicago, IL, 1985. Cottons; hand pieced, machine pieced, hand appliquéd, reverse appliquéd, and hand quilted. MAQS 1997.06.48

OPPOSITE, BOTTOM LEFT: **The Blade,** 62" x 84", Doreen Speckmann, Madison, WI, 1985. Cottons; hand pieced and hand quilted. MAQS 1997.06.06

OPPOSITE, BOTTOM RIGHT: **Mariner's Compass,** 78" x 90", Deborah Warren Techentin, Dunnellon, FL, 1985. Cottons; hand pieced and hand quilted. MAQS 1997.06.38

TOP: **Starburst,** 95" x 95", Judy Sogn, Seattle, WA, 1991. Cottons; machine pieced and hand quilted. MAQS 1997.06.75

BOTTOM: **Waste Not, Want Not,** 79" x 91", Louise Stafford, Bremerton, WA, 1990. Cotton blends; machine pieced and hand quilted. MAQS 1992.04.01

Pieced designs and their use are infinitely varied. A fascinating quilt can be made using only a single shape, such as the 1.5" x 2.5" strips stitched together in Louise Stafford's WASTE NOT, WANT NOT. Made of scraps gathered from others, this quilt involves over 6,975 pieces. Pieced quilts often feature designs that include several different standard geometric shapes, such as NOTHING GOLD CAN STAY, with its depiction of dandelions from birth through their "white hair" stage.

Often different pieced designs are used in the center and borders, as in MARINER'S COMPASS, with its Mariner's Compass center becoming a medallion center with several encircling borders composed of different shaped pieces. Judy Sogn's STARBURST features a center created using the Feathered Star pattern, with several borders, including one that seems to be folded because of the three-dimensional look added through use of color.

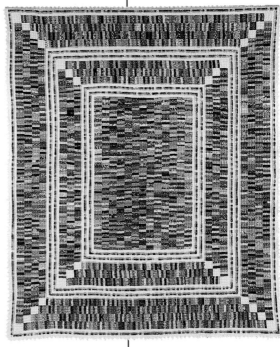

TOP: **Feathered Star Sampler,**
110" x 110", Imogene Gooch,
Rockville, IN, 1983. Cottons; hand
pieced and hand quilted.
MAQS 1997.06.21

BOTTOM: **Oriental Poppy,** 90" x 95",
Leureta Beam Thieme,
Pasadena, MD, 1987. Polished
cottons; machine pieced, hand
appliquéd, and hand quilted.
MAQS 1997.06.51

When shapes are being translated into quilt designs, they frequently involve curved areas. If there are substantial numbers of curves, or the shapes are very sharply curved, the quilt-maker will often select appliqué rather than piecing to construct those areas. As a result, many designs include both pieced areas and appliqué. In ORIENTAL POPPY the curving stems were added through appliqué after the blocks were pieced, and the details of the flower buds were added to COUNTRY GARDEN through appliqué as well. But gentle curves can also be pieced, as they are in DOUBLE WEDDING RING, a pattern often entirely pieced. The curves in SPLENDOR OF THE RAJAHS were machine pieced, using a pattern from *Curves Unlimited*, a book by Joyce Schlotzhauer, who taught many how to piece curves through her workshops and publications. In FEATHERED STAR SAMPLER several of the pieced stars at the centers create the illusion of curves.

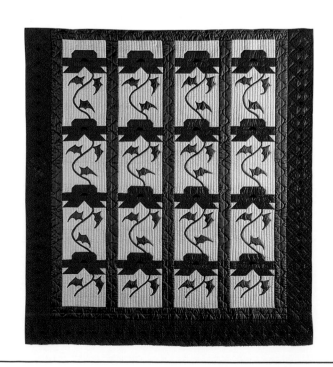

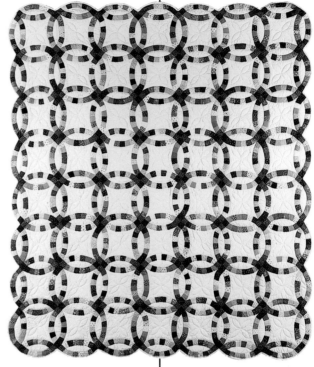

TOP LEFT: **Splendor of the Rajahs,**
84" x 106", Joyce Stewart,
Rexburg, ID, 1985.
Cottons; machine pieced and
hand quilted.
MAQS 1997.06.71

TOP RIGHT: **Double Wedding Ring,**
93" x 108", Claudia Dawson,
Harviell, MO, 1985. Cottons,
cotton polyester blends; machine
pieced and hand quilted.
MAQS 1997.06.18

BOTTOM: **Country Garden,**
80" x 96", Betty K. Patty,
Bradford, OH, 1985. Cottons;
machine pieced, hand appliquéd,
and hand quilted with trapunto.
MAQS 1997.06.14

CLOSE UP_____

In 1931, a number of
flower designs interpreted
in geometric shapes for
piecing were featured in
Ruby McKim's *101 Patch-work Patterns,* among
them the poppy pattern
used in ORIENTAL POPPY.
The curves in the flower
were suggested by shapes
that could be drawn on a
grid. McKim wrote:
"The pieced poppy is all
straight sewing, the sort
that may be run up on the
sewing machine, while the
bottom half of the block
has two leaves and a stem
that whips down by
hand."

CLOSE UP_____

A combination of sets is used in OLDE ENGLISH MEDALLION, which was based on an antique British quilt featured in *The Royal School of Needlework Book of Needlework and Embroidery*. This is a medallion quilt, a quilt with a major center design and a series of borders. The center is based on Mariner's Compass and Sunflower designs. Sunflowers have always been Cindy Vermillion Hamilton's favorite flowers. Appliqué is added, and then a border with corner squares. The next border involves Nine-Patch blocks set with Snowball blocks. This is followed by a border of strips cut from a printed floral border print that gives the appearance of different fabrics, with dark corner squares added. Next a series of appliquéd blocks set on point, so they are seen more as diamonds than as squares, are used, with triangles finishing them off as a strip. Notice how the measurements are exact enough that they run the length and width of the quilt, meeting perfectly at the corners! A second border like that on the other side of this strip is used, and then an elongated triangle design border with a scallop finishes the quilt.

The overall design of pieced quilts can be varied. If pieced blocks are set or positioned one right next to the other, the blocks are said to be "set solid," as in SQUARE WITHIN A SQUARE, WITHIN A SQUARE. The Log Cabin blocks with their light and dark halves formed around a center square or hearth, have been arranged to form an overall Barn Raising pattern as adjoining dark areas merge together, and light likewise, to create strips of color.

In FLOWER BASKET SAMPLER each block is separated from other blocks by strips of fabric called sashing. This set allows for framing each individual design. In AMISH EASTER BASKETS, four blocks are joined with sashing and a center square to create a larger block, and sashing and corner squares are used to set these.

OPPOSITE: **Olde English Medallion,**
104" x 104", Cindy Vermillion
Hamilton, Pagosa Springs, CO,
1992. Cottons; hand pieced, hand
appliquéd, and hand quilted.
MAQS 1992.22.01

TOP LEFT: **Flower Basket Sampler,**
90" x 112", Theresa Klosterman
Mooreton, ND, 1984.
Cottons, and cotton blends; hand
and machine pieced, hand
quilted, and hand embroidered.
MAQS 1997.06.23

TOP RIGHT: **Square within a Square
within a Square,**
102" x 102", Ruth Britton
Smalley, Houston, TX, 1986.
Cottons; machine pieced and
hand quilted.
MAQS 1997.08.01

BOTTOM: **Amish Easter Baskets,**
84" x 110", Elsie Vredenburg,
Tustin, MI, 1987.
Cottons; machine pieced and
hand quilted.
MAQS 1992.14.01

One of the design decisions a quiltmaker makes is how to finish the outer edges of a quilt – how much border to add, how to resolve the design in these areas. Sometimes quiltmakers use the overall design of the quilt all the way to the edge, or nearly to the edge with only a very narrow outer border, such as in TRIP AROUND THE WORLD. The outer border is often a piece of one of the fabrics used elsewhere in the quilt.

The outer borders in STARRY, STARRY NIGHT had to be redesigned because Mary Jo McCabe was running out of the floral striped fabric that had inspired her quilt. Sometimes an element from the pieced design in the center is used to create an outer border, as in PROSPERITY. Frequently a series of borders are added, like the wide white border with appliqué, followed by two narrow borders and one wider border of solid colors in BASKETS I.

TOP: **Trip Around the World,** 105" x 108", Mary Carol Goble, Nephi, UT, and Verla Hale Adams, Oakley, ID, 1985. Cottons and cotton blends; machine pieced and hand quilted. MAQS 1997.06.86

BOTTOM: **A Midwinter Night's Dream,** 99" x 99", Nancy Ann Sobel, Brooktondale, NY, 1988. Cottons; machine pieced, hand appliquéd, and hand quilted. MAQS 1996.01.17

OPPOSITE, TOP LEFT: **Starry, Starry Night,** 75" x 90", Mary Jo McCabe, Davenport, IA, 1985. Cottons; hand pieced and hand quilted. MAQS 1997.06.77

OPPOSITE, TOP RIGHT: **Baskets I,** 80" x 96", Wendy M. Richardson, Brooklyn Park, MN, 1984. Cottons; machine pieced, hand appliquéd, and hand quilted. MAQS 1997.06.04

OPPOSITE, BOTTOM: **Prosperity,** 84" x 84", Elaine M. Seaman, Kalamazoo, MI, 1985. Cottons; hand pieced, machine pieced, and hand quilted. MAQS 1997.06.59

Close Up_____

Nancy Ann Sobel's outer border in A MIDWINTER NIGHT'S DREAM is wide, with a variety of appliqué elements added. The quilt's center features an enlarged Crown of Thorns block with appliqué added to its large open shapes. For the outer border, a half snowflake appliqué like those in the center's appliqué is added. In the corner area of the border, small flowers, leaves, and scallops repeat those used around the center. The scallops join at each corner, with a last scallop curving across it.

HAND *Quilts*

TOP LEFT: **Night Bloom,** 56" x 72",
Jane Blair, Wyomissing, PA, 1985.
Cottons and cotton/polyesters; hand
pieced and hand quilted.
MAQS 1997.06.46

TOP RIGHT: **Oh My Stars,** 97" x 97",
Margie T. Karavitis, Spokane, WA,
1989. Cottons; hand pieced
and hand quilted.
MAQS 1992.15.01

BOTTOM: **Dot's Vintage 1983,**
84" x 100", Dorothy Finley,
Cordova, TN, 1983. Cottons;
hand appliquéd and hand quilted
with trapunto.
MAQS 1996.01.10

OPPOSITE: **Joie de Vie — Joy of Life,**
94" x 94", Candy Goff, Lolo, MT,
1998. Cottons; hand pieced, hand
appliquéd, and hand quilted.
MAQS 1999.01.01

The appliqué, piecing, and quilting in JOIE DE VIE were all completed by hand. Pieced by hand means that separate fabric shapes like the elongated triangles in the Mariner's Compass flowers were pieced together by hand using a running stitch. To the observer, the surface of a hand-pieced quilt does not look different from one pieced by machine because this stitching is only visible on the wrong side of the top. Sometimes people who hand piece the blocks will switch to machine piecing for the addition of long borders.

The flower, leaf, and stem elements of JOIE DE VIE were added with hand appliqué, using a nearly invisible slip or appliqué stitch along the folded edge. This results in the observer seeing only a fabric shape against a background, with no visible stitching. A very different look is achieved with machine appliqué, which usually involves stitching on the surface of the appliqué shape.

The quilting, the stitching that goes through all layers, was also done by hand, stitch-by-stitch with a single thread passing with each stitch from the surface of the quilt to the back. The result is a slight puckering of the quilt's surface.

Quilts made entirely by hand continue to be made, in all styles and by all types of makers. NIGHT BLOOM is composed of rows of hand-pieced traditional Basket of Scraps blocks – one row in one direction and the next in the opposite one. Hand quilting creates a brick design behind them. DOT'S VINTAGE 1983 is one of many quilts that Dorothy Finley has made entirely by hand to build a collection of future heirlooms. In accordance with the custom of keeping humankind's work from suggesting perfection, she has omitted a grape from one of the quilt's clusters, and embroidered on the back "A bird ate the missing grape." The traditional star blocks and diamond borders in OH, MY STARS were hand pieced by Margie T. Karavitis, and the elaborate quilting design also added completely in hand stitching. Hand piecing is found to be more relaxing by some quilters, and can also be more easily carried to different locations, or done while watching television or talking with friends.

When quiltmakers speak of creating their handmade quilts, they often speak of rewarding work and a striving for the best they can produce. Sometimes a contest is the incentive, as was a Mountain Mist contest for BED OF PEONIES. Karin Matthiesen feels her handworkmanship is her greatest strength in quiltmaking. Dorothy Mackley Stovall decided early on that she would "strive for quality rather than quantity" and finds that the results of handwork please her more than her machine work; STAR BRIGHT, with its 1,510 fabric pieces, was also inspired by a Mountain Mist contest.

Julia Overton Needham, who won a blue ribbon with the first quilt she entered in competition, uses shows and competitions as a learning experience. TENNESSEE PINK MARBLE, with its intricate hand quilting, was named for the marbleized pink and green fabric used in the outer border. RISING MOONS is entirely hand pieced and hand quilted.

TOP: **Star Bright,** 81" x 96", Dorothy Mackley Stovall, Livingston, MT, 1985. Cottons; hand pieced and hand quilted. MAQS 1997.06.74

BOTTOM: **Stella Antigua,** 91" x 91", Hanne Vibeke de Koning-Stapel, Bilthoven, Holland, 1988. Silks; hand pieced and hand quilted. MAQS 1993.03.01

OPPOSITE, TOP: **Rising Moons,** 73" x 67", Elaine Stonebraker, Scottsdale, AZ, 1988. Cottons; hand pieced and hand quilted. MAQS 1997.06.64

OPPOSITE, BOTTOM LEFT: **Bed of Peonies,** 85" x 96", Karin Matthiesen, Madison, WI, 1986. Cottons; hand appliquéd and hand quilted. MAQS 1996.01.04

OPPOSITE, BOTTOM RIGHT: **Tennessee Pink Marble**, 72" x 88", Julia Overton Needham, Knoxville, TN, 1990. Cottons; hand pieced and hand quilted. MAQS 1996.01.26

CLOSE UP_____

Striving for just the right effect sometimes involves changing plans for a quilt. STELLA ANTIGUA was designed to be an octagonal table cover. Hanne Vibeke de Koning-Stapel began hand piecing its Lone Star center on a sailing trip with her husband and son that began in Antigua. When the table cover was finished her husband didn't like it, so it was turned into a quilt, using a hand-pieced variation of the center star at the corners, Virginia Stars in the borders, and much hand quilting.

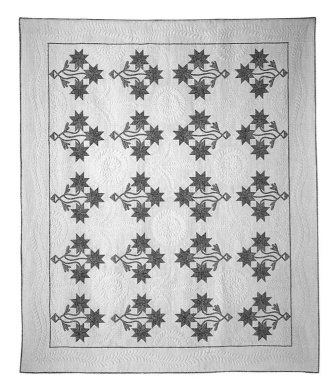

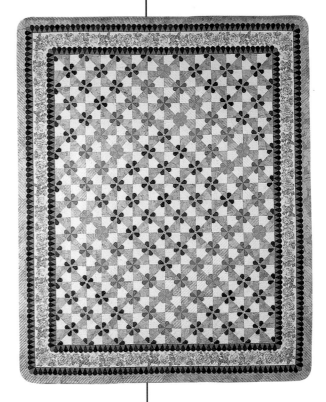

TOP LEFT: **Quilted Counterpane,**
72" x 100", Patricia Spadaro,
Delmar, NY, 1985. Polished
cotton; hand quilted.
MAQS 1997.06.60

TOP RIGHT: **Nosegay**, 36" diameter,
Judy Simmons, Marietta, GA,
1986. Cottons; hand appliquéd
(including broderie perse)
and hand quilted.
MAQS 1997.06.47

BOTTOM: **Lilies Are Forever,** 76" x 88",
Carole Steiner, Santa Maria, CA,
1994. Cottons; machine pieced,
hand appliquéd, and hand quilted.
MAQS 1996.01.15

OPPOSITE, TOP: **Rococo Islands,** 94" x
94", Mary Jo Dalrymple, Omaha,
NE, 1982. Cottons; hand pieced
and hand quilted.
MAQS 1993.01.01

OPPOSITE, BOTTOM: **Le Jardin de Nos
Reves,** 68" x 88", Myrl Lehman
Tapungot, Cagayan de Oro, Philip-
pines, 1997. Cottons; hand quilted
with trapunto and hand embroidered.
MAQS 1997.01.01

Designs in quilts are created in various ways. Patricia Spadaro's QUILTED COUNTERPANE is what is referred to as a whole-cloth quilt, a one-fabric quilt in which the entire design is communicated through the quilting stitches, in this case done by hand with no thimble over a period of 11 months. Hand-pieced blocks provide much of the design for ROCOCO ISLANDS, which includes an original design repeated eight times and a traditional Mariner's Compass block at the center. In Carole Steiner's hand-stitched quilt LILIES ARE FOREVER, hand-pieced Carolina Lily blocks are combined with hand appliqué and hand quilting to create a special quilt to honor her twentieth wedding anniversary. It's appliqué that Judy Simmons loves, so hand-appliquéd flowers and ribbons abound in NOSEGAY. Roses are created using *broderie perse*, a technique that involves cutting printed images from fabric and appliquéing them in place on a quilt.

CLOSE UP_____

A myriad of hand techniques add endless detail to LE JARDIN DE NOS REVES, which was inspired by vintage molded ceiling designs. Ten quilters worked with Myrl Lehman Tapungot for over seven months to complete the quilt. In addition to hand quilting, there is trapunto or stuffed work – areas with additional stuffing added to create dimension. These areas were stuffed with colored yarns to add subtle shading. Hand-embroidered details include butterflies and other creatures, with "fairy dust" added to emphasize their energy.

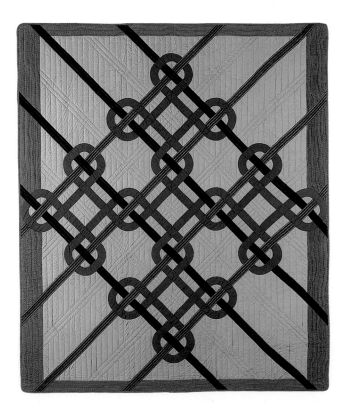

Handmade quilts often link past and present. In NE'ER ENCOUNTER PAIN, Mary Golden randomly combined 1980's calicoes with 1880's prints. The quilt's handwork calmed her during a period when her husband was diagnosed with a brain tumor. Chris Kleppe enjoys quiltmaking because it draws on a long folk tradition. MALTESE CROSS uses the embroidery pattern of the same name; Kleppe found it "immensely gratifying to spend hundreds of hours constructing one fine object."

Arlene Statz enjoys working with variations on patterns of the past as well; in CLAMSHELL the designs of the same name were hand appliquéd to strips of fabric, which were then pieced together. Growing up on a farm, Louise Stafford says quilting was one of the many required "chores." Now, making hand-stitched quilts brings memories of earlier "chores," but is also fun, right down to adding the tiny hand-embroidered flowers at the feet of the COLONIAL LADY. Beverly Mannisto Williams made VICTORIAN FANTASY OF FEATHERS AND LACE in 1986 to commemorate her twenty-fifth wedding anniversary. Its making later became connected with the Challenger disaster. Williams was quilting the background that day, and noticed a missing flower, which she left missing as a remembrance of this tragic event.

OPPOSITE, TOP LEFT: **Clamshell,** 84" x 104", Arlene Statz, Sun Prairie, WI, 1984. Cottons; hand appliquéd, machine pieced, and hand quilted. MAQS 1997.06.11

OPPOSITE, TOP RIGHT: **Colonial Lady,** 87" x 120", Louise Stafford, Brewerton, WA, 1984. Cotton and cotton blends; hand pieced, hand appliquéd, hand embroidered, and hand quilted. MAQS 1997.07.04

OPPOSITE, BOTTOM: **Maltese Cross,** 76" x 88", Chris Kleppe, Milwaukee, WI, 1987. Cottons; hand and machine pieced and hand quilted. MAQS 1997.06.35

TOP: **Victorian Fantasy of Feathers and Lace,** 89" x 104", Beverly Mannisto Williams, Cadillac, MI, 1986. Cotton, handmade bobbin lace edge; hand quilted. MAQS 1996.01.29

BOTTOM: **Ne'er Encounter Pain,** 90" x 90", Mary Golden, Gloucester, MA, 1982. Cottons; hand pieced and hand quilted. MAQS 1997.06.42

CLOSE UP_____

To make VICTORIAN FANTASY OF FEATHERS AND LACE, Beverly Mannisto Williams marked her quilting design on a 90" piece of muslin fabric. Light brown thread was used to hand stitch the quilting designs and off-white for the background grid. The edging is bobbin lace that Williams also made by hand. The quilting in this piece involved about 2,000 hours and the lace 300.

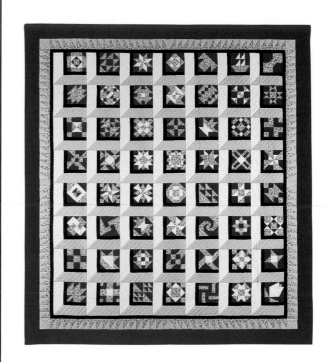

The hand-pieced and hand-appliquéd designs of Jane Blair blend the old and the new, looking traditional to some viewers, and innovative to others. GYPSY IN MY SOUL manipulates the traditional Queen Charlotte's Crown block, with plain blocks and appliqué added, along with unique coloration. SATURN'S RINGS isn't based on a traditional pattern, but does grow out of the resourcefulness so much a part of the quilt-making tradition. Inspired by television photos of Saturn's rings, Susan Knight searched her kitchen for plates and pot lids that could be used to draw the pattern for this quilt.

En route home from the annual AQS Quilt Show, several members of the Trigg County Quilter's Guild decided to make a group quilt to enter the next year, and TRADITION IN THE ATTIC, with its many hand-pieced traditional blocks, was the result. A local contest inspired Lillian J. Leonard to hand stitch TRANQUILITY. She dreams of quilting patterns and wishes she had "the time to carry out all these visions." The center medallion is an enlarged version of the two-patch surrounded by Flying Geese.

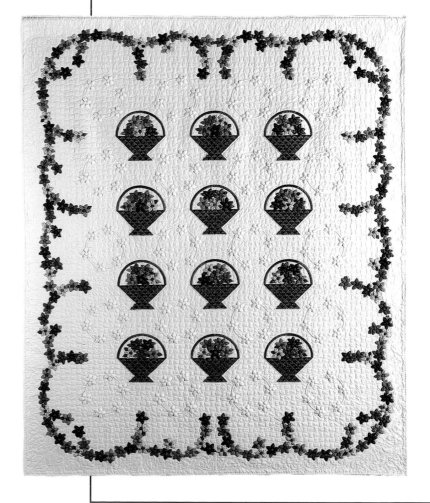

OPPOSITE, TOP LEFT: **Tranquility,** 78" x 92", Lillian J. Leonard, Indianapolis, IN, 1986. Cottons; hand pieced, hand appliquéd, and hand quilted. MAQS 1997.06.85

OPPOSITE, TOP RIGHT: **Tradition in the Attic,** 86.5" x 94.5", Trigg Co. Quilters, Cadiz, KY, 1988. Cottons; hand pieced and hand quilted. MAQS 2000.05.01

OPPOSITE, BOTTOM: **Spring Flower Baskets,** 88" x 103", Janice Streeter, Virginia Beach, VA, 1989. Cottons; machine pieced, hand appliquéd, and hand quilted. MAQS 1996.01 23

TOP: **Gypsy in My Soul,** 66" x 84", Jane Blair, Wyomissing, PA, 1987. Cottons and cotton/polyesters; hand pieced, hand appliquéd, and hand quilted. MAQS 1996.01.12

BOTTOM: **Saturn's Rings,** 61" x 41", Susan Knight, Bay Village, OH, 1986. Cottons and linen; hand pieced, hand appliquéd, and hand quilted. MAQS 1997.06.68

CLOSE UP____

SPRING FLOWER BASKETS brings together three of its maker's loves: Prairie Points, baskets, and the Star Flower pattern. This quilt's baskets are formed from Prairie Point strips hand stitched together, with appliquéd handles. The baskets are filled with Star Flowers, with gathered and stuffed petals. A white-on-white Star Flower corded wreath block is alternated with the basket blocks, and additional appliquéd Star Flowers encircle the center.

TOP: **The Beginnings,** 64" x 84",
Dawn Amos, Rapid City, SD, 1990.
Cottons, hand dyed; hand
appliquéd and hand quilted.
MAQS 1996.01.05

OPPOSITE, TOP LEFT: **Strawberry
Sundae,** 70" x 84", Laverne N.
Mathews, Orange, TX, 1986.
Cottons and cotton blends; hand
appliquéd and hand quilted.
MAQS 1997.06.78

OPPOSITE, TOP RIGHT: **Reach for the
Stars,** 66" x 82", Jan Lanahan,
Walkersville, MD, 1986. Cottons,
flannels, satins; hand pieced
and hand quilted.
MAQS 1997.06.61

OPPOSITE, BOTTOM LEFT: **Morisco,**
80" x 90", Jane Blair, Wyomissing,
PA, 1984. Cottons and
cotton/polyester blends; hand
pieced and hand quilted.
MAQS 1997.06.40

OPPOSITE, BOTTOM RIGHT: **Night and
Noon Variation,** 72" x 92", Joyce
Ann Tennery, Oak Ridge, TN,
1987. Cottons; hand pieced
and hand quilted.
MAQS 1997.06.45

Dawn Amos was inspired to make her hand-stitched quilt THE BEGINNINGS as a tribute to her start as a quiltmaker. Her first machine quilt had been a Broken Star design and her first appliqué quilt, made for the Statue of Liberty Contest, began with an eagle. Joyce Ann Tennery wanted a block that would furnish her with 6" center squares so she could create different miniature blocks for those spaces. The result was NIGHT AND NOON VARIATION. Jan Lanahan hand stitched REACH FOR THE STARS as a tribute to the Challenger crew and their families. Jane Blair is often inspired by a desire to combine the old and the new. MORISCO incorporates large, small, rectangular, square, and half blocks of the traditional Bleeding Heart design.

CLOSE UP_____

It was through her interest in antique quilts that Laverne N. Mathews became inspired to make her hand-stitched STRAWBERRY SUNDAE. She had collected antique quilts and visited museums to see them. It was at the French Trading Post Museum in Beaumont, Texas, that she saw the model for this quilt.

TOP: **Night Flowers,**
60" x 60", Deborah Lynn Ward
(1952 – 1991), Arroyo Grande,
CA, 1991. Cottons; machine
pieced, machine appliquéd, hand
beaded, and machine quilted.
MAQS 1992.19.01

BOTTOM: **Aletsch,**
81" x 41", Michael James, Lincoln,
NE, 1990. Machine pieced and
machine quilted.
MAQS 1997.06.01

MACHINE Quilts

The MAQS collection celebrates a wide range of techniques, including quilts that are made using sewing machines. The sewing machine has been in use since the 1860s, and was used with the making of quilts by some needleworkers once it was available in private homes. Early on sometimes just a small amount of machine work was used on the surface of the quilt, as a proud indication that the maker owned a machine and had developed proficiency.

In NIGHT FLOWERS, machine appliqué and quilting with black thread further the nighttime theme. The fabric colors and patterns in RESTORING THE BALANCE, DISTANT CLOSENESS, and ALETSCH are seen in their purity, in part because of their machine quilting. Often done "in the ditch" or hidden close to the seamlines, machine quilting adds none of the puckering and resultant shadows that hand quilting does.

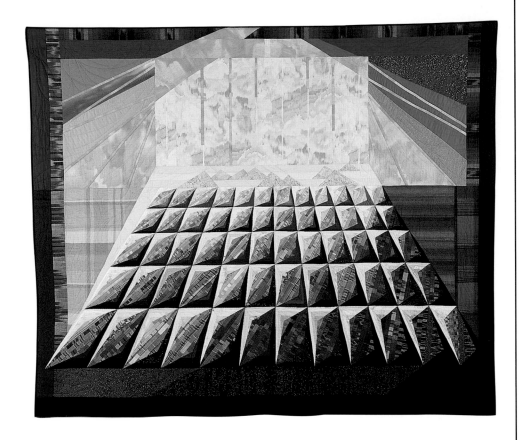

TOP: **Restoring the Balance,**
95" x 80", Alison Goss,
Durango, CO, 1990. Cottons and
poly-cotton blends; machine pieced
and machine quilted.
MAQS 1992.08.01

BOTTOM: **Distant Closeness,**
75" x 50", Solveig Ronnqvist,
Exeter, RI, 1986.
Cottons and satins; machine
pieced, machine appliquéd, hand
appliquéd, and machine quilted.
MAQS 1997.06.17

CLOSE UP_____

In ALETSCH, Michael James tries to capture his sensory responses to the vast mountainous basin in the Swiss Alps that encloses the Aletsch Glacier, the largest in western Europe. He comments: "What impressed me most was the very audible sound of millions of gallons of water rushing unseen beneath the perfectly still expanse of glacier. It seemed incongruous: the unrelenting movement of so much water and the stony rigidity of so much ice."

TOP LEFT: **Hot Fun,** 56" x 63," Melody Johnson, Cary, IL, 1995. Hand-dyed cottons; machine embroidered, fused, and machine quilted.
MAQS 1996.01.14

TOP RIGHT: **Springtime Sampler,** 108" x 108," Lois T. Smith, Rockville, MD, 1986. Cottons; machine pieced and machine quilted.
MAQS 1997.06.72

BOTTOM: **Ohio Bride's Quilt,** 81" x 81," Debra Wagner, Cosmos, MN, 1989. Cottons; machine pieced and machine quilted with trapunto.
MAQS 1997.06.49

OPPOSITE, TOP: **Ancient Directions,** 80" x 67," Alison Goss, Durango, CO, 1990. Cottons; machine pieced and machine quilted.
MAQS 1996.01.02

OPPOSITE, BOTTOM: **Corona II: Solar Eclipse,** 76" x 94," Caryl Bryer Fallert, Oswego, IL, 1989. Hand-dyed fabrics; machine pieced and machine quilted.
MAQS 1996.01.07

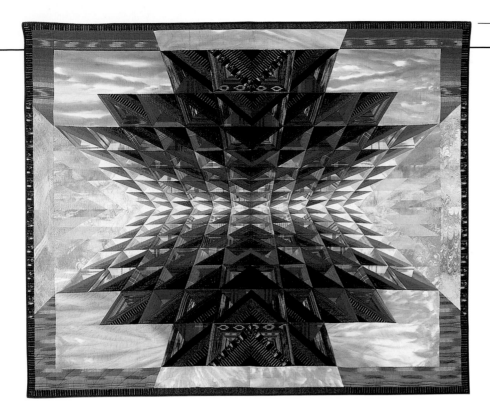

CLOSE UP_____

The central image of
ANCIENT DIRECTIONS
was drafted in mirror-
image perspective, and
each small section was
machine pieced to paper,
using a method Alison
Goss had developed.

This quilt was selected as
one of the Best 100
American Quilts in the
20th Century. Seven quilts
in the MAQS collection
were so honored. See
page 134 for a list.

A milestone in twentieth-century machine quiltmaking occurred in 1989 when Caryl Bryer Fallert's quilt CORONA II: SOLAR ECLIPSE won the then $10,000 cash award for Best of Show at the AQS Quilt Show & Contest in Paducah, Kentucky. This marked the first time a totally machine-stitched quilt had won the Best of Show award at this national quilt show.

Quiltmakers like Lois T. Smith had been teaching and writing about machine making quilts for some time and one of her machine-stitched quilts had won Best of Show/Masters Division at the 1988 AIQA Show in Houston. Quiltmakers specializing in machine work, such as Debra Wagner, had also been participating in national shows, but many quiltmakers were still dismayed when a quilt that was not at least in part hand stitched won the AQS award.

Quiltmakers have continued to explore machine techniques. HOT FUN and its AQS Quilt Show award helped Melody Johnson promote the use of fusible web with her machine techniques. It is her hope its use will "increase the ease and speed of construction and completion of art quilts which we hope will lead to more originality and better design."

TOP LEFT: **Indian Summer,** 106" x 106," Sherry Sunday, New Kingston, PA, 1993. Cottons; machine pieced, hand appliquéd, and machine quilted. MAQS 1997.07.13

TOP RIGHT: **Kettle Moraine Star,** 91" x 91", Diane Gaudynski, Pewaukee, WI, 1996. Cottons; machine pieced and machine quilted. MAQS 1997.02.01

BOTTOM: **Hammered at Home,** 77" x 78", Iris Aycock, Woodville, AL,1994. Cottons; machine pieced and machine quilted. MAQS 1996.01.13

OPPOSITE, TOP: **Heliacal Rise,** 71" x 74", Laura Murray, Minneapolis, MN, 1996. Cottons and silks; hand painted, machine pieced, and machine quilted. MAQS 1997.03.01

OPPOSITE, BOTTOM: **Goato and Friends,** 83" x 83", Barbara Barber, Andover, Hants, England, 1995. Cottons; machine appliquéd, machine quilted, and machine embroidered. MAQS 1996.02.01

INDIAN SUMMER, with its elaborate machine appliqué and quilting, was made in remembrance of Sherry Sunday's daughter's passage from childhood into womanhood. It includes a poem on the back written by Sunday's daughter. GOATO AND FRIENDS, with its machine appliqué, reverse appliqué, embroidery, and quilting, was inspired by a goat (named Goato) that lived across the field from Barber and her family and inspired many family walks.

The title of HELIACAL RISE, a quilt that includes both hand and machine piecing, refers to the astronomical term used to describe two stars coming very close together, forming what appears to be one large star. The totally machine-made KETTLE MORAINE STAR was inspired by many handmade antique Amish and Mennonite quilts.

CLOSE UP_____

For HAMMERED AT HOME, fresh leaves were literally "hammered" on a cotton fabric that had been treated with a mordant to help it accept the dye. Paulownia, sweetgum, Christmas ferns, kiwi, and tulip poplar leaves were used. The imprinted fabric was treated with a fixative and lines were inked to emphasize veins. Solid color borders were dyed with other plants.

In 1993, for the first time at the AQS Quilt Show, a major award was given to recognize excellence in machine workmanship. The winner of that first Bernina-sponsored award was Debra Wagner for her quilt FLORAL URNS. The existence of this award signified the increase in activity and art in this field. Debra went on to win this award a second time during her quiltmaking career.

Another quiltmaker has also won this prestigious award more than once. Diane Gaudynski is a four-time winner with stunning quilts including BUTTERNUT SUMMER, SWEETHEART ON PARADE, and OCTOBER MORNING. With today's quiltmakers, machine quiltmaking continues to be taken to new heights.

CLOSE UP_____

Mary L. Hackett spontaneously constructed FEAR OF THE DARK using a variety of black fabrics, some cut into tiny strips, to make 460 blocks. Hackett then chose 256 for the quilt. Adrift in the floating colors and patterns are a few of the fears that crop up at night. On the back Hackett placed a giant pieced Log Cabin block, a reference to the quilts "traditional parentage."

OPPOSITE, TOP: **October Morning,** 82" x 82", Diane Gaudynski, Pewaukee, WI, 1999. Cottons; machine pieced, machine quilted with trapunto, and machine broderie perse. MAQS 2000.03.01

OPPOSITE, BOTTOM: **Butternut Summer,** 81" x 81", Diane Gaudynski, Pewaukee, WI, 1998. Cottons; machine pieced and machine quilted. MAQS 1999.02.01

TOP: **Floral Urns,** 90" x 90," Debra Wagner, Cosmos, MN, 1992. Cottons; machine pieced, machine appliquéd, machine embroidered, and machine quilted. MAQS 1996.01.11

BOTTOM LEFT: **Fear of the Dark,** 87" x 87", Mary L. Hackett, Carterville, IL, 1993. Cottons; machine pieced and machine quilted. MAQS 1997.07.10

BOTTOM RIGHT: **Sweetheart on Parade,** 82.5" x 83", Diane Gaudynski, Pewaukee, WI, 1997. Cottons; machine pieced and machine quilted. MAQS 1998.03.01

CLOSE UP_____

THE BEATLES QUILT was made by sisters Pat Holly and Sue Nickels, to celebrate their memories of this music group whose songs filled their teenage years. The quilt's layout was inspired by an antique folk art quilt with a Tree of Life center. Everything in this machine-stitched quilt has meaning, from the apples representing their recording label to the many appliqué blocks that each represent a different record album released by this group. Four album blocks surrounding the tree represent each of the four Beatles, with hands and guitar symbols surrounding their names and birth dates.

OPPOSITE, TOP LEFT: **One Fish, Two Fish, Red Fish, Blue Fish,** 82" x 92", Laura Heine, Billings, MT, 1993. Cottons; machine pieced and machine quilted. MAQS 1996.01.21

OPPOSITE, TOP RIGHT: **Discovery,** 18.5" diameter, Francelise Dawkins, Queensbury, NY, 1991. Silks; machine appliquéd, machine embroidered, and machine quilted. MAQS 1997.07.07

OPPOSITE, BOTTOM: **The Beatles Quilt,** 95" x 95", Pat Holly and Sue Nickels, Muskegon and Ann Arbor, MI, 1998. Cottons; machine appliquéd, machine pieced, and machine quilted. MAQS 1998.01.01

TOP & DETAIL BELOW: **Escapade,** 80" x 80", Libby Lehman, Houston, TX, 1993. Cottons, rayon and metallic thread; machine pieced, machine embroidered, and machine quilted. MAQS 1997.07.09

Quiltmakers are ever exploring the possibilities that fabric and thread — and machine work — offer. Using only one fish design that is squeezed into a variety of sizes and shapes, Laura Heine created ONE FISH, TWO FISH, RED FISH, BLUE FISH. Working with yards and yards of decorative threads, Libby Lehman stitched machine embroidered ribbons curling in fascinating ways over the surface of her pieced quilt top ESCAPADE. Her embroidered ribbons are transparent in the way that layered watercolors often are. Francelise Dawkins has developed a technique she calls "silkollage," which she used in DISCOVERY. It involves four layers of material that are machine quilted, appliquéd, embroidered, or painted on.

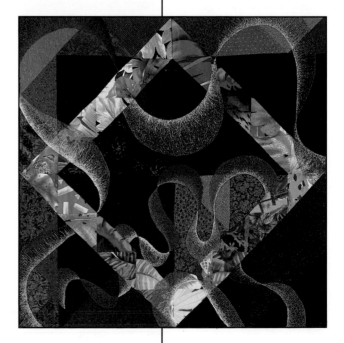

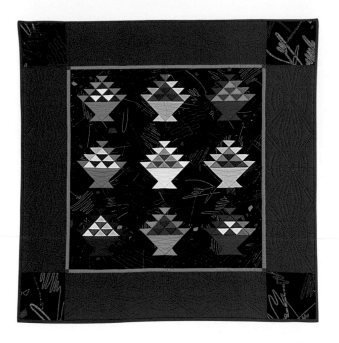

SPECIAL
Techniques

In the same way that quiltmakers creatively incorporate all types of fabrics in their works, they are ever incorporating new techniques, some borrowed from other arts, some made possible by new products and equipment. What was planned as a New Year's Eve quilt by Joyce Stewart became a more general CELEBRATION quilt, and its wild fabrics inspired Joyce to add glittering rhinestones as embellishments. Hallie H. O'Kelley was inspired by an abundance of colorful zinnias in her garden to use screen printing to place ZINNIAS IN THE WINDOWS OF MY LOG CABIN. The Log Cabin blocks are composed of fabrics she had hand dyed, in an original arrangement.

GRACE is built of hand-painted, torn fabrics that have been machine appliquéd to a base. It is part of a series in which Erika Carter uses these techniques to create landscapes that become personal narratives. Stylized hands among the rectangles at the foot of the trees suggest a path, and trees lean over, protecting the traveler.

TOP: **Celebration,** 46" x 46", Joyce Stewart, Rexburg, ID, 1988. Cotton; machine pieced and machine quilted. MAQS 1992.11.01

BOTTOM: **Grace,** 45" x 69", Erika Carter, Bellevue, WA, 1993. Hand painted and commercial cottons; machine appliquéd and machine quilted. MAQS 1997.07.11

OPPOSITE, TOP & DETAIL: **Precipice,** 75" x 93", Jan Myers-Newbury, Pittsburgh, PA, 1989. Hand dyed cottons; machine pieced and machine quilted. MAQS 2001.08.01

OPPOSITE, BOTTOM: **Zinnias in the Windows of My Log Cabin,** 77" x 85", Hallie H. O'Kelley, Tuscaloosa, AL, 1987. Cottons; machine pieced and hand quilted. MAQS 1997.06.34

CLOSE UP_____

Jan Myers-Newbury, long known for her hand dyeing of fabric for quilts, considers PRECIPICE a "threshold piece" for a new way of thinking and working. For twelve years Myers-Newbury had been piecing together tiny bits of fabric, mostly solid pieces, to create design. She had experimented with creating a linear design using some leftover pieces of "scrunch-dyed" fabrics and realized she could intentionally create a pattern in fabric by folding and binding a large piece of fabric – a blue-violet fabric was the beginning of PRECIPICE. Design decisions were made in response to this heavily patterned fabric. Myers-Newbury comments: "PRECIPICE has a spiritual quality for me, though I did not set out to create this. The piece seems to divide itself between heaven and hell, and its upward movement presents hope."

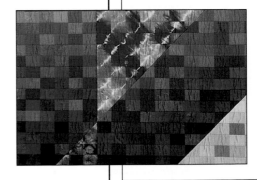

There are many special techniques used for piecing and appliquéing quilts. There is a tradition of creating quilts using many small pieces – creating a design in much the same way that cross-stitch x's or a computer screen's pixels do. Cletha Bird saw a photograph of a very famous quilt by Grace Snyder created in tiny triangles and decided to create her own FLOWER BASKET using 42,680 half-inch (finished size) triangles.

Chizuko Hana Hill's GREAT AMERICAN ELK quilt consists of 19,500 three-quarter inch squares, stitched together bargello style. When her husband saw the completed quilt top, he liked the back better, with its many seam allowances creating surface texture. After two weeks' deliberation, Hill finished the quilt with the seamed side becoming the "right" side.

Another traditional technique used to create quilts with many small pieces is Seminole piecing, which involves piecing strips of fabric together and then cutting across them to create strips of small pieces. This technique was used to "build" the outer baskets in BASKETS AND THE CORN. Jan Lanahan then hand painted the coiled basket in the center using dyes. JELLY BEAN was the first in Angela W. Kamen's series of quilts that include sheer sections. The backing and batting are cut out of some areas, to allow the organza pieces to become "windows."

OPPOSITE, TOP LEFT: **Great American Elk,** 65" x 70", Chizuko Hana Hill, Garland, TX, 1996. Cottons; machine and hand pieced, hand quilted. MAQS 1998.05.01

OPPOSITE, TOP RIGHT: **Flower Basket,** 95" x 100", Cletha Bird, Columbus, IN, 1987. Cottons and cotton blends; machine pieced and hand quilted. MAQS 1997.06.22

OPPOSITE, BOTTOM: **Baskets and the Corn,** 67" x 80", Jan Lanahan, Walkersville, MD, 1986. Cottons and linens; embroidered, hand painted, machine pieced, and hand quilted. MAQS 1992.07.01

TOP: **Traditional Bouquet,** 52" x 66", Ludmila Uspenskaya, New York, NY, 1995. Cottons; machine appliquéd and machine quilted. MAQS 1995.01.01

BOTTOM: **Jelly Bean,** 57" x 77", Angela W. Kamen, Bedford Corners, NY, 1998. Cottons and silk organza; machine pieced, machine quilted, machine embroidered and couched. MAQS 1998.02.01

CLOSE UP

In Ludmila Uspenskaya's TRADITIONAL BOUQUET, fabric pieces with printed images of flowers are machine appliquéd to fabric, with their raw edges left exposed. The resulting bouquet is wondrously integrated. For the vase containing her flowers, Uspenskaya has applied paints, air brushing the vase to suggest its rounded surface. To this appliquéd quilt surface she has then added her signature quilting, parallel rows that add visual texture. Uspenskaya brings to quiltmaking her own unique style. A graduate of the Mukhina Art School in St. Petersburg, Russia, Uspenskaya moved from what she called fabric collages to working with large scale textile installations in public buildings. She began quilting in 1989 when she responded to an invitation from the All Russia Museum of Decorative, Applied, and Folk Art to submit a quilt for an exhibit. She brought to her work her experience with large scale textiles and a visual arts background, and developed her quiltmaking style while fairly isolated from the work of other contemporary quiltmakers. In 1995 she moved to the United States and her work was featured in its first one-person exhibit at MAQS.

TOP LEFT: **Stained Glass Windows,**
98" x 112", Nadene Zowada,
Buffalo, WY, 1986.
Cotton/polyester; hand appliquéd.
MAQS 1997.06.73

TOP RIGHT: **Hearts & Stars,**
40" x 48", Judy Seidel,
Ft. Collins, CO, 1985. Cottons
and cotton blends; hand and
machine pieced, hand quilted.
MAQS 1997.06.28

BOTTOM: **Neon Nights,** 53" x 53",
Moneca Calvert, Reno, NV, 1987.
Cottons, cotton blends; machine
pieced and hand quilted.
MAQS 1997.06.43

OPPOSITE, TOP: **Up, Up, and Away,**
79" x 79", Laura Crews-Lewis,
Cape Girardeau, MO, 1985.
Cottons, chintz; hand appliquéd,
hand quilted, and stuffed
and Seminole pieced.
MAQS 1997.06.89

OPPOSITE, BOTTOM: **Indiana Crazy,**
70" x 71", Linda Karel Sage,
Morgantown, IN, 1988. Cottons
and blends; machine and hand
pieced, hand appliquéd, hand painted, hand embroidered, hand quilted.
MAQS 1997.06.30

In the hands of the quiltmaker a particular traditional pattern can be used in special ways. Moneca Calvert's work has resulted in an "updating" of the traditional Clamshell pattern. In NEON NIGHTS she pieces large Clamshell shapes in gradated colors, using them to create a bordered medallion quilt. Also note her careful cutting of a border print fabric for use in various sections of the design.

Patterns for stained glass were enlarged to make STAINED GLASS WINDOWS. With this special appliqué technique, the leading for the stained glass is created by bias strips of black fabric. Trapunto, the technique of quilting a design and then inserting additional stuffing from the back to make the area raised, can be used for wonderful effects in quiltmaking. The center hearts in HEARTS & STARS and many areas of UP, UP, AND AWAY were enhanced using this special technique.

CLOSE UP_____

The star points in INDIANA CRAZY are created in the special technique traditionally used for crazy quilts. In this technique, irregularly shaped pieces are stitched to a larger shape of fabric, often muslin. Crazy quilts were frequently composed of square or rectangular blocks. In this quilt the foundation shape was a large triangle. Linda Karel Sage included among her patches an Inko-Dye photo of her mother, who taught her to sew. In a traditional crazy quilt fancy embroidery stitching would likely have been used along the edges of fabric pieces.

Special techniques in quiltmaking often involve using materials in different ways. In A LITTLE BIT OF CAN-DLEWICKING Bonnie K. Browning adds Cluny lace, satin ribbon, and candlewicking to her white-on-white quilt. In candlewicking, embroidery stitching, usually involving Colonial knots, is completed using heavy white candlewick thread.

In SHADOW BALTIMORE BRIDE Marion Shenk employs shadow appliqué. She cut shapes from bright fabrics, lays them on a white background, and then covers the entire surface with a thick voile fabric. The colors show through, but softened. Using embroidery floss, she stitches the two layers together, securing the fabric shapes. To the casual observer the shapes look as though they had been appliquéd to the surface.

Fascinated by the stencil-painted quilts of the 1820s, Marie Sturmer has taught and written books about this technique, and used it to create the designs in RIBBONS AND ROSES.

Janice Anthony used fiber-reactive dyes to paint the fabrics for her quilt INCANTATION.

OPPOSITE, TOP: **Ribbons and Roses**, 72" x 86", Marie Sturmer, Traverse City, MI, 1989. Cotton; stenciled, hand embroidered, and hand quilted. MAQS 1997.06.63

OPPOSITE, BOTTOM LEFT: **Incantation**, 29" x 44", Janice Anthony, Jackson, ME, 1985. Cottons, painted silk; hand and machine pieced, and hand quilted. MAQS 1997.06.29

OPPOSITE, BOTTOM RIGHT: **A Little Bit of Candlewicking**, 64" x 97", Bonnie K. Browning, Paducah, KY, 1986. Unbleached muslin, Cluny lace and satin ribbon; candlewicked, machine pieced, and hand quilted. MAQS 1997.06.33

TOP: **Shadow Baltimore Bride**, 86" x 102", Marion Shenk, Scottdale, PA, 1986. Cotton broadcloth, voile and cotton embroidery floss; hand quilted. MAQS 1997.06.70

BOTTOM: **A Mandala of Flowers**, 76" x 81", Noriko Masui, Saitama, Japan, 1997. Cottons, silks, polyesters, and materials from Japanese kimono and obi; hand pieced, hand appliquéd, and hand quilted. MAQS 1998.04.01

CLOSE UP

Noriko Masui was inspired by Tibetan sand mandalas to create her own mandala – a graphic mystic symbol of the universe to be used as an aid to meditation – of pieced and appliquéd flowers. Her mandala achieves a fascinating illusion of dimension, a special effect found in quite a number of traditional blocks. The effect is achieved through the overall design and the use of values in fabric choices.

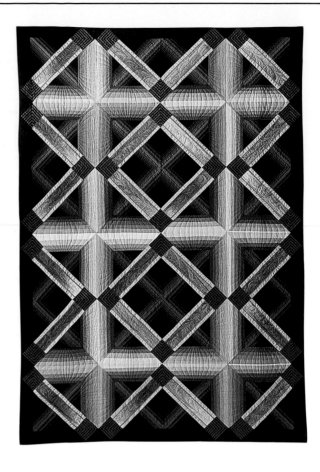

TOP LEFT: **Night Beacons III,** 48" x 67", Vicki L. Johnson, Soquel, CA, 1991. Cottons; painted and machine appliquéd. MAQS 1992.12.01

TOP RIGHT: **Diffractions III,** 65" x 94", Mary Morgan, Little Rock, AR, 1989. Hand-dyed cottons; machine pieced and hand quilted. MAQS 1997.06.16

OPPOSITE, TOP & DETAIL: **Migration #2,** 88" x 88", Caryl Bryer Fallert, Oswego, IL, 1995. Cottons; dye painted, hand dyed, machine pieced, machine appliquéd, and machine quilted. MAQS 1996.01.18

OPPOSITE, BOTTOM: **Crossings,** 64" x 52", Cynthia Buettner, Hilliard, OH, 1986. Hand-dyed cottons; machine pieced and hand quilted. MAQS 1997.06.15

Beginning in the 1980s, hand-dyed fabrics in graduated colors began to be created by quiltmakers for their own work, and/or sold in combinations for other quiltmakers to be used. CROSSINGS was made by Cynthia Buettner using the first of the hand-dyed fabrics that she later has sold to quilters and shops around the world. Dyed in steps of color darkness, these fabrics are often combined in quilts to produce illusions of depth or dimension.

Mary Morgan explored with the use of such fabrics to create depth in DIFFRACTIONS III, a quilt she began in a workshop with Nancy Crow. Vicki L. Johnson's quilt NIGHT BEACONS III uses hand-painted and hand-marbled fabrics to create a Pigeon Point Lighthouse scene. The ocean, planets, and moon are also painted.

CLOSE UP_____

The center fabric and outer border fabrics in MIGRATION #2 were painted with fiber-reactive dyes. Across the quilt fly curving strips of the traditional Flying Geese pattern (triangles) and machine appliquéd more realistic geese. Caryl Bryer Fallert created these shapes on her computer, modifying scans of bird photos. Caryl has been a leader in the use of computer software for quilt design. The machine quilting adds another design element. Feathered Plumes intertwine with the flying geese, and organic patterns fill the outer border. Inside each triangle representing a flying bird, is a more realistic quilted image. Caryl drew these and then quilted them by machine, but the other quilting designs were added freehand, with no marking of the quilt top. When Caryl is quilting, she is quilting on a standard sewing machine, manipulating the entire three-layer quilt!

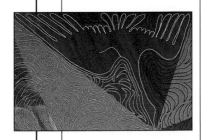

TOP: **Cabins in the Cosmos,**
50" x 55", Lonni Rossi,
Wynnewood, PA, 1998.
Commercial, hand dyed, surface
designed cottons, gold lamé,
computer chips, aviation artifact;
machine pieced, machine stitched,
and fused.
MAQS 1999.03.01

BOTTOM: **Terrarium,** 40" x 50.5",
Marion Huyck, Chicago, IL, 1985.
Cottons; hand pieced, machine
pieced, hand appliquéd, reverse
appliquéd, and hand quilted.
MAQS 1997.06.82

Embellishments, additions to the surface, are one way that quilters often add meaning to their works. Lonni Rossi embellished the surface of CABINS IN THE COSMOS with 18 computer memory chips and an aviation artifact from the fuselage section of a Douglas DC-3 to suggest that her artist and philosopher "Log Cabin colony" floating in outer space could serve as a beacon of communication.

Marion Huyck added beadwork to TERRARIUM to suggest sun shining on the flowers below. In REFLECTION #3, Caryl Bryer Fallert uses tucks of fabric to create a changing visual effect. Two-sided fabric tucks, with different colors on each side, are pieced into a patterned background, so the piece changes as the viewer walks from one side to the other.

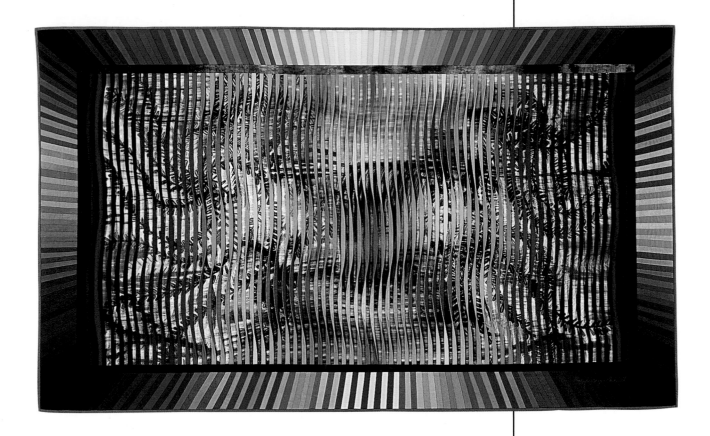

CLOSE UP_____

MANY STARS was created on a piece of muslin fabric using a batik method. Each star shape was painted in melted wax on muslin fabric, using a paper cut design.

The fabric piece was then submerged in a vat of blue dye with borax added to finalize the process. The areas covered with wax remained white. The wax was then removed using an iron and newsprint.

TOP: **Reflection #3,** 77" x 45", Caryl Bryer Fallert, Oswego, IL, 1990. Hand-dyed, hand-painted fabrics; machine pieced and machine quilted.
MAQS 1997.07.15

BOTTOM: **Many Stars,** 77" x 96", Mary E. Kuebler, Cincinnati, OH, 1987. Cottons; batiked and hand quilted.
MAQS 1997.06.36

TOP: **Barking Up the Wrong Tree,**
58" x 45", Sharon, Malec, West
Chicago, IL, 1999. Cottons and
cotton blends; hand painted,
machine appliquéd, machine
couched, and machine quilted.
MAQS 2000.04.01

BOTTOM: **DRESDEN GARDEN,** 85" x 86", Paul
D. Pilgrim, Oakland, CA, 1992; quilted by
Toni Fisher, Belton, MO. Cottons and 1940's
Dresden Plate blocks; hand pieced, hand
appliquéd, machine pieced, and hand quilted.
MAQS 1997.05.17

Quiltmakers can have a great deal of fun employing their special design techniques.

Sharon Malec was inspired by the 2000 AQS Quilt Show's "dogwood" theme to make BARKING UP THE WRONG TREE. Malec had made many "dog" quilts, several of which were hanging on her wall. And she had just completed a quilt depicting a large sequoia tree, which was also hanging on the wall. The idea just clicked to combine the two to fit the theme. She spent much time fitting the images of dogs in her trees – there are a total of five.

In DRESDEN GARDEN Paul D. Pilgrim had fun combining 1940's Dresden Plate and Grandmother's Flower Garden blocks, two designs he would never have made himself. Pilgrim enjoyed incorporating "orphan" blocks he had purchased in antiques shops and at flea markets.

CLOSE UP

In partnership with Gerald E. Roy for 33 years, the late Paul D. Pilgrim developed one of the foremost collections of quilts in the country. As they traveled around the country, Paul found he just couldn't leave behind many of the stacks of "orphan" blocks he found in shops – the quilt blocks that had been completed but never found their way into any quilt. After completing a quilt from blocks left by his grandmother, he expanded the custom of using inherited pieces, incorporating in his work "orphan blocks" made by anonymous quiltmakers from the past.

MAQS:
The Second Decade

O ver the years since MAQS opened I have watched enthusiastically as it carved out a special niche in the quilt world. The museum has sought out exhibitions which represent the breadth and depth of quiltmaking as an art and craft that moves into the twenty-first century. Striving for a balance of respect and interest in the quiltmakers who have preceded today's enthusiasts, the exhibits have taken a look back as well as a look forward. The policy of hosting vintage and historic quilts has satisfied those visitors who relish the quilts of our heritage. Contemporary quiltmakers have found inspiration and admiration in the quilts that spur greater experimentation with the techniques and technology which give today's quilters new and exciting tools with which to create new work.

Ongoing efforts by invited quiltmakers to meet the Pilgrim/Roy Challenge each year have continued to support MAQS both financially and in increased national visibility. After the year of travel and exhibit, the quilts return to MAQS to be auctioned. This provides an opportunity to own a quilt made by a prominent quiltmaker and proceeds benefit the museum.

Workshops presented by nationally known instructors underscore MAQS's commitment to broaden the skills of participants. The MAQS workshop format gives students an opportunity to spend several days working with their instructor.

Many of the goals projected by a long-range planning conference called "Envision Our Future" have been met and others continue to be implemented. I am honored to be serving on an effective board which steadfastly moves MAQS forward to meet new challenges, gain increased independence, and continue to honor today's quilters.

Bettina Havig
Member MAQS Board of Directors

LEFT: **SNOW SCAPE,** 72" x 62", Jo Diggs, Portland, ME, 1995; MAQS 2004.02.01

ACQUISITIONS
Advisory Board

T he Museum of the American Quilter's Society established an advisory committee that included three board members, two staff members, and three national advisory members. The advisors bring to the annual meetings broad and in-depth experiences teaching, judging, and running businesses related to American quilt activities.

The first major project was to select contemporary quilts by quiltmakers who were not represented in the MAQS collection. Ten quilts were selected and exhibited during the 10th Anniversary celebration of the Museum of the American Quilter's Society.

Their quilts represent the contributions of these women through their vision of going beyond tradition and introducing remarkable creativity with the use of color, design and fabric choices.

Helen Thompson
MAQS Acquisitions
Advisory Board Member

TOP LEFT: **Enlightenment,** 85" x 85", Vicki Hallmark, Austin, TX, 2001. Cottons, polyester and metallic threads; machine pieced, machine appliquéd, and machine quilted. MAQS 2001.11.01

TOP RIGHT: **Indian Barn Raising,** 86" x 96", Becky Herdle, Rochester, NY, 1988. Cottons; machine pieced and hand quilted. MAQS 2001.14.01

BOTTOM: **Blue Earth Filled with Water and Flowers,** 76" x 83", Keiko Miyauchi, Nagano, Japan, 2001. Hand dyed cottons, polyester; hand appliquéd, trapuntoed, and hand quilted. MAQS 2001.12.01

OPPOSITE, TOP: **Pop Stars,** 86" x 86," Philippa Naylor, Dhahran, Saudi Arabia, 2002. Cottons, machine pieced, trapuntoed, and machine quilted MAQS 2002.03.01

OPPOSITE, BOTTOM: **Who's Your Poppy?,** 61" x 62", Claudia Clark Myers, Duluth, MN, 2001. Cottons; machine paper pieced, machine appliquéd, machine embroidered, and machine quilted. MAQS 2002.02.1

CLOSE UP_____

POP STARS is Philippa Naylor's updated version of a Feathered Star design, and she found it a "wonderful challenge" to piece precisely. Philippa accomplished this by drawing a full-sized pattern and then tracing it to provide a template for each piece.

Since the first edition publication of this book, MAQS has continued to expand the Founder's Collection of contemporary quilts, a collection that now numbers over 200. Each quilt added since 2001 represents the highest standards of quiltmaking excellence. As chronicles of ever-evolving trends in color, design, and technique, most have come to the museum as purchase prizes through the prestigious annual competitions of the American Quilter's Society: ENLIGHTENMENT (2001) by Vickie Hallmark, and POP STARS (2002) by Philippa Naylor, Machine Workmanship Award; BLUE EARTH FILLED WITH WATER AND FLOWERS (2001) by Keiko Miyauchi, Hand Workmanship Award; WHO'S YOUR POPPY? (2002) by Claudia Clark Myers, Best Wall Quilt. Becky Herdle's INDIAN BARN RAISING became part of the collection by means of a generous donation.

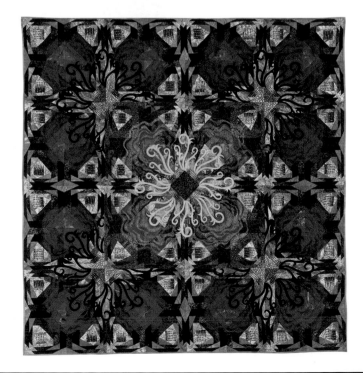

Quilts can be traditional or contemporary, but regardless of their category or the technique used to create them, all quilts in the Founder's Collection are exquisitely rendered artistic expressions in fabric. Many of these quilts represent purchase awards from the American Quilter's Society's annual competitions, such as Suzanne Marshall's MOTHER'S DAY, winner of the 2002 Hand Workmanship Award, and Inge Mardal's IT'S NOT SUMMER YET, 2001 Best Wall Quilt. However, a prize-winning quilt artist may elect to keep their quilt and forfeit the cash award, as happened with Best of Show winners in 2001 and 2002. Ever-increasing cash awards are offered in hopes that the best quilts from each year's competition can be shared with quilt lovers from around the world.

TOP: **It's Not Summer Yet,** 54" x 41", Inge Mardal, Brussels, Belgium, 2001. Cottons; hand appliquéd, machine embroidered, and machine quilted.. MAQS 2001.13.01

BOTTOM: **Mother's Day,** 81" x 81", Suzanne Marshall, Clayton, MO, 2001. Cottons; hand appliquéd, hand embroidery, and hand quilted. MAQS 2002.01.01

CLOSE UP_____

Suzanne Marshall spent three years creating MOTHER'S DAY. She finished appliquéing the green borders of each block before deciding what images would fill them. Scherenschnitte designs worked perfectly. During the 1800s Scherenschnitte (pronounced shair-en-shnit-teh), was a popular folk art practiced among Swiss-German immigrants settling in the Pennsylvania area. Scherenschnitte, which literally means "scissors-cutting," was a craft used to decorate birth and marriage certificates, shelf paper, and holiday decorations.

TOP & DETAIL: **Lime Light,**
81" x 81," Philippa Naylor,
Dhahran, Saudi Arabia, 2003.
Cottons, machine pieced,
trapuntoed,
and machine quilted
MAQS 2003.01.01

BOTTOM, RIGHT: **Blueberry Morning,**
85" x 85", Cynthia Schmitz,
Arlington Heights, IL, 2003.
Cottons; machine pieced,
trapuntoed,
and machine quilted.
MAQS 2003.02.01

BOTTOM, LEFT: **Complimentary Composition,**
64" x 65", Gerald Roy,
Warner, NH, 1998/1999.
Cottons; machine pieced,
and machine quilted.
MAQS 2004.01.01

The American Quilter's Society celebrated its 20th Anniversary Quilt Show & Contest in Paducah in April 2004. Linda M. Roy's SPICE OF LIFE was the Hancock's of Paducah Best of Show winner. THE SPACE QUILT by Sue Nickels and Pat Holly was awarded the Bernina Machine Workmanship Award. Winner of the RJR Fabrics Best Wall Quilt Award was Inge Mardal's SUN-BATHING BLUE TIT. Best of Show winner of the first contest in 1985 was Katherine Inman's ORIENTAL FANTASY, page 32.

TOP: **Totem,** 62" x 50", Gabrielle Swain, Watauga, TX, 2003. Cottons; machine pieced, hand appliquéd, hand embroidery and hand quilted. MAQS 2003.04.01

BOTTOM: **Star Flower,** 83" x 83", Elsie M. Campbell, Dodge City, KS, 2003. Cottons; machine pieced, machine appliquéd, and hand quilted. MAQS 2003.03.01

CLOSE UP_____

Although completely machine made, the design of THE SPACE QUILT was inspired by folk art quilts of the mid- to late 1800s. Documenting the U.S. manned space program, it was made as a tribute to the quilters' father who was a World War II Air Force pilot and test pilot in the 1950s.

TOP RIGHT: **Sun-Bathing Blue Tit,** 66" x 80", Inge Mardal, Chantilly, France, 2004. Cottons; hand painted and machine quilted. MAQS 2004.01.03

TOP LEFT: **The Space Quilt,** 87" x 87", Sue Nickels, Ann Arbor, MI, and Pat Holly, Muskegon, MI, 2004. Cottons, polyester and metallic threads; machine pieced, machine appliquéd, and machine quilted. MAQS 2004.01.02

BOTTOM: **Spice of Life,** 82" x 82", Linda M. Roy, Pittsfield, MA, 2004. Cottons; metallic thread and perle cotton embroidery; hand appliquéd and hand quilted. MAQS 2004.01.01

QUILTMAKER *Profiles*

*N*othing ever stands still or stays the same.
In quilting we have seen remarkable changes –
stunning innovations and experiments
as quilters stretch themselves and
their imaginations to embrace new concepts.

– Virginia Avery
from *Wonderful Wearables*

Verla Hale Adams made her first quilt in 1934, while planning her marriage. With quilting frames placed on chair backs and tied with strips of strong cloth, Adams made this quilt, and many more over the years for her ten children. She learned much about quilting at the Relief Society of the Church of Jesus Christ of Latter Day Saints. For a number of years her daughter, Mary Carol Goble, furnished "beautiful pieced quilt tops," so Adams could complete the quilting and binding.

Dawn Amos began quilting in 1978 when her oldest son was just a year old. She explains. "I wanted to be able to stay home with my son and still earn some money. My husband's family is Sioux Indian and they had made and sold star quilts for some time. His family helped me make my first quilt, which was a Broken Star." Amos continued making and selling star quilts for many years. Her first appliqué quilt was made for the Statue of Liberty contest, and early on she began dyeing her own fabrics.

Virginia Avery made her first dress when she was 12, teaching herself to sew on a treadle machine. In high school she received a Japanese kimono, which inspired interest in clothing and using exotic fabrics. She sewed through college and created her working wardrobe. While raising her family she taught sewing in shops, and then in the 1960s learned to quilt. As interest in appliqué and garments flourished, she became internationally known, lecturing, teaching, and writing many books.

Iris Aycock made a few quilts in the early 1970s, to make colorful bed coverings for her children. Her mother had made quilts as gifts. Aycock didn't make any more quilts for many years, and then began again, first making bed quilts, then wall quilts, and then framed pieces. Quilting has since changed from a hobby to being a full-time occupation for her. Juried into the Southern Highland Craft Guild in 1995, she exhibits and sells her work at the guild's fairs and shops.

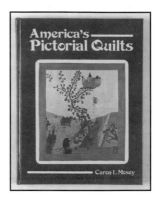

Charlotte Warr Andersen learned to sew from her mother while she was young and has continued to enjoy quiltmaking. She made her first quilt, a Log Cabin, shortly after her marriage in 1974. Pictorial quilts are her specialty, with original, one-of-a-kind designs ranging from highly realistic appliqué to abstract piecing. Andersen teaches quiltmaking, is a charter member of AQS, and has written two books on pictorial appliqué. She enjoys making quilts connected with American history.

Faye Anderson, a Chicago native, majored in graphic design at the University of Denver and then for ten years ran a women's clothing store and a fabric store in Breckinridge, CO. Enjoying the advertising and layouts she did for her stores, she eventually became art director for a magazine serving five Colorado ski areas. In 1980 she moved to Denver, took a sampler class, and began quilting. Anderson is active as a teacher and has authored a book on needle-turn appliqué.

Janice Anthony began quilting in 1975, after painting for 15 years. Her first quilts were geometric and traditional, but from the outset she was interested in the interplay of light and dark, and in expression through color. She learned about traditional techniques from a group of accomplished Maine quilters. Janice finds it a challenge to translate ideas and designs into fabric because of the technical difficulties of piecing curved lines and because colors in fabric interact differently than colors in paint.

Artists from *America's Pictorial Quilts*, Caron Mosey (coordinator), Carolyn Muller, Lois K. Ide, Helen Kelly, Pat Cox, Barbara Crane, Paula Nadelstern, Dawn Rappold, Rhoda Cohen, Victoria Faoro, Susan Turbak, Lee Farrington, Jean Johnson, Masami Kato, Linda Cantrell, Elly Dyson, Art Salemme, Erma Martin Yost, Carole Adams, Joan Schulze, Judy Mathieson, Roberta Horton, Chris Wolf Edmonds, Elaine Sparlin, Ronnie Durrance, Mona Barker, Cathy Grafton, Ed Larson (w/Sarah Hass), Steve Schutt, Donna Makim, Gwen Marston, Joe Cunningham, Shannie J. Coyne.

Barbara Barber began quilting in 1991 to make a quilt for her bed. She is self-taught and the quilts she makes for exhibition may take 6 – 12 months. Quilting is a full-time occupation, with her time divided between her own work, teaching, lecturing, and writing. Barber's husband, Peter, assists with her quiltmaking, producing accurate geometrical drawings from her rough designs. Barber's teaching has taken her to Europe and the US, and she is author of a book and two videotapes.

Cletha Bird explains that a photograph of a very famous quilt by Grace Snyder inspired her to make her own Flower Basket quilt. Cletha comments, "What a challenge this project was for a first quilt – to try to create something that even resembled this accomplished quiltmaker's work would be quite an achievement. Had I known more about the challenges of quiltmaking, I am sure that I would not have tried that design!" Quilting is now an essential part of Cletha's life.

Jane Blair, a professional quilt artist and teacher living in Wyomissing, PA, specializes in new design possibilities developed from traditional patterns. She is self-taught and has devoted an eight-hour day to quilting since 1972. Retired, she has taught quiltmaking and designing in the Philadelphia area since 1976 and has taught and lectured in many states. Her quilts, seen in magazines, exhibits, and how-to books, have made her known to quilters everywhere.

Judi Warren Blaydon is a quilt artist, author, and teacher whose quilts have been in numerous national and international exhibitions. Her work is in public and private collections in the U.S., Japan, and Australia and has been featured in *Eighty-eight Leaders of the Quilt World Today* (Nihon Vogue 1995) and in Robert Shaw's *The Art Quilt*. Her book, *Fabric Postcards: Landmarks and Landscapes, Mountains and Meadows* (AQS) is both a practical guide and a uniquely personal travel memoir.

Quiltmaker *Profiles*

*Q*uiltmaking is a wonderful form of artistic expression. New methods of exploration are discovered all the time, yet there is still plenty of room for very traditional approaches. I hope that quiltmaking and the appreciation of quilts stay around for many years to come.

– Nancy S. Brown

Arleen Boyd first became interested in quiltmaking in 1980 when she saw her husband's aunt working on what she now realizes was a "quilt-as-you-go" project. Boyd had always enjoyed sewing, so she took two continuing education quilt classes. She enjoyed the way that quilting combined the pleasures of sewing with designing. At the close of the first class, the group decided they didn't want to stop quilting together so they formed a quilt group that has continued to meet ever since.

Becky Brown grew up in Kansas with the "warmth and security" of sleeping under quilts made by her grandmother. Becky explains, "At age eight she invited me to join her at the quilting frame. There was never a suggestion that quilting was something one learned; it was simply something one did. As the years passed, my interest in quilting and design progressed. At last, I had found the way to release the silent voice within me, blend it with basic skills, and like my grandmothers, leave it as my gift to the future."

Moneca Calvert has been a quiltmaker of original contemporary designs since 1982. Her quilts have been exhibited, awarded, and published nationally and/or internationally. GLORIOUS LADY FREEDOM won the California State and Grand Prize in the 1986 Great American Quilt Contest and has been included in the 100 Best American Quilts of the Twentieth Century. Calvert loves teaching/lecturing, judging, and all facets of the quilt world.

Elsie Campbell grew up with a needle in her hand in the small Mennonite community of Deer Creek, Oklahoma. After graduating from Northwestern Oklahoma State University at Alva, she taught home economics, music, and special education in public schools. She began exhibiting her quilts nationally in 1992 and has won several prestigious awards.

Nancy S. Brown's mother taught her to quilt. She states that she liked the idea of creating something that might last a long time and the fact that she could create a large design without requiring a lot of space. Her first quilt was an original design of several scenes with penguins that took two years. Nancy prefers making animal portrait quilts using appliqué, but she occasionally makes quilts based on old family photographs, to celebrate and remember.

Bonnie K. Browning learned to sew as a child from her mother, Mary Kirkland, but it was in 1979, when she retired as executive secretary of Mercy Hospital in Davenport, IA, that she began to quilt. She started teaching quiltmaking in 1985, became an NQA certified quilt judge, and has since taught around the world. Browning has written five books on quilting. In 1994 she moved to Paducah, KY, to become show chair for AQS.

Barbara Brunner sewed for her daughters when they were young, but as they became older, she turned to quilting and lost interest in other crafts. Quilting has given Brunner a way to express her feeling and ideas through handwork. She comments, "I love flowers, especially roses and tulips. I do not have an actual flower garden myself, so all my flowers are found on my quilts." Brunner, who has been quilting for years, tries to quilt every day.

Cynthia Buettner's fascination with quilting began when as a child she slept under a Grandmother's Fan quilt made by her great-grandmother, who was described as a "master" quilter. Having completed her first quilt in 1982, Buettner was soon teaching quilting and designing her own patterns. Although many quilts preceded and followed her quilt in the MAQS collection, it remains an important quilt. It was made of the first of the hand-dyed fabrics she sold around the world.

Canyon Quilters of San Diego is a non-profit group established in 1985 by area women who wished to meet and share their quilting knowledge and skills. Thirty women from the guild appliquéd, pieced, and embroidered the quilt in the MAQS collection, working from a design by Donalene Rasmussen and fabric she had selected. Guild members also completed the quilting, and the resulting quilt generated many donations. It also provided a great sense of satisfaction for participants.

Erika Carter has been making contemporary quilt art since 1984. Nature is often the inspiration for her imagery, expressed texturally through use of color, pattern, piecing, and hand quilting. Carter has studied with nationally known instructors, including Roberta Horton, Katie Pasquini Masopust, Nancy Halpern, and Nancy Crow. Her quilts have been featured in such shows as Quilt National and the annual AQS Show, and are in collections in the U.S. and Europe.

Mary Chartier is a National Quilting Association (NQA) certified teacher and has been quilting since the early 1970s. Chartier believes quiltmakers should make quilts to suit themselves, and "not worry whether judges will like the design, the colors, the fabrics." But Chartier adds about her own quiltmaking: "I know I do a better job technically in the piecing and the appliquéing when I know that a judge is going to be examining my quilt."

Nancy Clark has happy childhood memories of her grandmother's dairy farm in Tucson. Memories of the smell of desert rain and being able to see great distances stayed with her as she lived in the cities of the East and Midwest. The Clarks moved to Phoenix in 1958 after she had completed a degree in home economics education at Iowa State and a degree in veterinary medicine. Later Nancy completed a master's degree in textiles and clothing at Arizona State University.

QUILTMAKER
Profiles

I feel proud that the museum's founders wanted STELLA ANTIGUA for the MAQS collection. They stressed that this would be the first collection quilt made by a non-American quilter, which of course made me feel especially honored.

– Hanne Vibeke de Koning-Stapel

Barbara Lydecker Crane's designing and making of art quilts come from a lifelong interest in sewing, her college degree in fine arts, and her former profession as a graphic designer. Crane comments, "I wish to convey my reverence for the natural world, with all its wonders and mysteries. Birth, regeneration, migration, water, and sky especially fascinate me. My work contains strong central imagery and patterns, to parallel my belief that only a calm, centered self can experience wonder."

Laura Crews-Lewis learned quilting at an early age from her mother. Laura comments, "I feel that my choice of a design career was prompted by my childhood love of paper dolls (which I still have). My quilting, in turn, is influenced by my design training." The quilt in the MAQS collection was Crews-Lewis's first original effort. The stuffing technique was her own, and she later continued to perfect it. The overall concept for the quilt was inspired by an Oriental rug seen in a book.

Jo Diggs has cut, stitched, and loved fabric since childhood. Her appliqué landscapes, wearable art, and serene multi-layer scenes span several decades. Jo concentrates primarily on landscapes but does an occasional fish or floral quilt. Having taught throughout North America, Jo values creativity in both her own work and her students' work. She loves fabric and layers it to create scenic views, flashy fish, and floral appliqués. She travels and teaches extensively, always calling Portland, Maine, home.

Adabelle Dremann, after many years of teaching art, began making original pictorial quilts in 1985. Adabelle recalled the first quilts she made, "As a bride I made my first two quilts that went to the county fair and won blue ribbons. Night quilting was done by the light of a kerosene lamp, on the lap hoop bought from Sears and Roebuck." Adabelle's son comments, "Mother enjoyed anything artistic, and was also a great lover of travel. It's a shame she hadn't enough time to put all of her many ideas into quilts."

Mary Jo Dalrymple was born in Little Rock, Arkansas. As a child she was taught embroidery and needlepoint and loved music. She graduated from North Texas University. While pursuing a career as an orchestral musician, she became fascinated by quilting and later studied at the Arkansas Arts Center Museum School. She has numerous publications and exhibits to her credit. Dalrymple comments, "My overall goal is to live and work both as deeply and as lightly as I can."

Francelise Dawkins, a native of Paris, France, with Caribbean ancestry, has been living in the U.S. since 1977. She initially worked as a translator and taught French as well as French Caribbean folk dancing. After taking a fiber arts course at the Art League School of Indianapolis in 1985 and moving to New York City in 1987, she has become a nationally exhibited textile artist. Her work has been featured in a number of exhibits and publications, and she gives lectures on her collage techniques.

Claudia Dawson became interested in quilting when she was about 13 years old, as she watched her mother make quilts for the family's beds. Dawson speaks of her own quiltmaking: "The first quilt I made was a Nine Patch, which I did by hand. When my sewing skills improved, I started making more and more complicated patterns. Making quilts later became a hobby that filled the time while my husband was working away from home on the railroad."

Hanne Vibeke de Koning-Stapel fell in love with quilts while on vacation in the U.S. at a bed and breakfast in Vermont. She tried quilting on her own, but became frustrated. Then she took instruction from Sophie Campbell in Paris, France, in 1978. In 1981 de Koning-Stapel began teaching, and was a pioneer instructor in Holland. She is author of one book in Dutch about machine patchwork and quilting and *Silk Quilts* (The Quilt Digest Press).

Patricia Eaton is a teacher and freelance writer. Eaton comments, "After spending the last 18 years involved in making quilts, teaching, writing, reading, and dreaming about quilts – I can truly say that quilts have become my prime interest and they have led me into a life I would not have otherwise known." Eaton adds, "I love the act of making quilts, and the people I have met through quilting, teaching, and writing have added many blessings and much excitement to my life."

Chris Wolf Edmonds lives in Kansas at the eastern edge of the tall grass prairie. "Here," she says, "the eye is not distracted by majestic miracles of mountain, redwood, or sea. In fact it is their absence that makes the majesty of great expanses evident. Earth and sky are a kaleidoscopic palette of hue, value, and chroma swaying to the cadence of the seasons. The ceaseless subtle consonance of color is a symphony of inspiration and wonder: the rhythm of my existence and the stimulus for my art."

B.J. Elvgren is a folk artist working in the textile medium. A love of fabric and skill in sewing led her to begin quilting in 1979. Using fabric as her palette, this self-taught artist creates appliquéd and quilted pictures. Elvgren's works are exhibited throughout the U.S. and are in many private collections. A recipient of numerous honors, she received a PA Arts Council Fellowship award in 1987. Her work is enriched by a strong folk heritage and is a celebration of the wholeness of God's creation.

Linda Goodmon Emery has been a quilter since 1975 and specializes in original design quilts. Her works have won numerous awards, and she is an NQA Master Quilter, and the author of *A Treasury of Quilting Designs.* Her quilts have been featured in several quilt magazines and books. Emery encourages quiltmakers to "set goals high and keep pushing to reach them – you never know what you are capable of achieving unless you try."

QUILTMAKER
Profiles

A beautiful quilt can be done by hand or
by machine, and a machine-quilted quilt is
not necessarily one that is inferior, fast, and
sloppy, but a "different" way to create a beautiful
quilt by taking the same care and effort
in doing it as in doing the finest handwork.

– Diane Gaudynski

Jean M. Evans, a retired art educator, works with the same energy and commitment when creating original art quilts from her paintings and drawings as does her identical twin, Joyce Murrin. Evans prefers bold colors, strong contrast, curved lines, figures, faces, and often a subtle sense of humor. Her award-winning, published quilts are hand appliquéd and hand quilted with occasional embellishments.

Caryl Bryer Fallert is internationally recognized for her art quilts, which are distinguished by their colors and multi-level illusions of light and motion. Her attention to detail has earned her a reputation for fine craftsmanship as well. She is a three-time winner of the Best of Show Award at the AQS Quilt Show. Fallert's quilts have appeared in numerous national and international publications and her work is in public, museum, corporate, and private collections. Fallert lectures and conducts workshops for quilt and textile arts groups

Mary Carol Goble has always been fascinated with quilts. Her first was a Nine Patch she made for her doll when a little girl. Goble has been making all types of quilts for some years. She comments, "Quiltmaking is fascinating to me because I am continually learning something new about it." For a number of years Goble pieced quilt tops for her mother, Verla Hale Adams, to quilt and bind. The MAQS collection quilt is one of these pieces.

Candy Goff, who had sewed since childhood, began quilting in 1986 when she made a baby quilt. Self-taught, she relied on books and magazines for inspiration and information. Then in 1993 she visited the AQS Quilt Show and MAQS. She explains that seeing "such exquisite quilts in the cloth" inspired her subsequent career in quiltmaking. Her quilts have won major awards, but she continues to remember it is important to make quilts you love, not just quilts to please the judges.

Hazel B. Reed Ferrell, a native of West Virginia, recalls, "walking four miles to attend a one-room school." Ferrell comments: "I cannot remember not being involved in sewing as I was the only girl in a family of four." She learned quilting and sewing from her mother and grandmother and they were "a necessity as well as a tradition." Ferrell's quilts are in museum collections. She has received many awards and has published a quilt book, *Down Home Needle Art to the Museum Walls*.

Dorothy Finley's interest in quiltmaking began when in 1974 her husband brought her an armload of quilting books. She put her knitting aside and thumbed through them to please her husband and the result has been a prolific quilting career. Her goal is to build a collection of future heirlooms by making quilts from old patterns for future generations to see and appreciate. Her quilt in the MAQS collection has been awarded Masterpiece status by the National Quilting Association.

Donna Duchesne Garofalo began quilting in 1980, shortly after the birth of her third child. Her first project was a bed quilt for one of her daughters. Using this medium, she could combine her previous interests in painting and sewing. Garofalo learned to quilt with a friend, and in the 1980s quilting became a major part of her life and a source of income. Having taken a full-time job in 1989, she made her last wallhanging in 1991 but plans to soon resume her professional work in quilting.

Diane Gaudynski grew up sleeping under her grandmother's scrap quilts. She has been making quilts herself since 1980 and machine quilting them since 1988. A self-taught quiltmaker, she uses the Harriet Hargrave method for machine quilting. Gaudynski is a four-time winner of the machine workmanship award at the AQS quilt show, and her quilts have been featured in numerous publications and shows. She also teaches, lectures, and writes on quiltmaking techniques.

Mary Golden began quiltmaking in 1972 with the repair of an old family quilt. This project led to antique quilt restorations and sales, which in turn led to appraisals, quiltmaking, teaching, and lecturing. By 1974 Golden had become a state juried artist and teacher for the League of New Hampshire Craftsmen. She is the author of *The Yankee Friendship Quilt* and illustrator of original floral and Kaleidoscope designs. Her quilts have appeared in publications and exhibits, and she lectures and teaches.

Imogene Gooch's mother taught her to quilt when she was a teenager. Years later she was thankful for those quilting lessons when she was recovering from back surgery. Using her mother's leftover scraps, she pieced a Thousand Pyramids quilt top and was hooked. She made her first contest quilt in 1976 for an Indianapolis Star Flower and Garden contest. Gooch has won many quilting awards, is an NQA certified teacher, and has several quilts in the Stearns and Foster Collection.

Irene Goodrich began piecing a patchwork quilt top when she was four years old, and completed it by the time she started school. She completed her second top at the age of 13, but both remained tops until she was in her forties. Quilting became "serious business" for Goodrich in 1967 when she decided to make a quilt for each person in her family. Since then, she has won Best of Show awards at the Ohio State Fair, as well as many other awards.

Alison Goss grew up in northern California, earned a B.A. from Mt. Holyoke College (MA), and teaching credentials from the University of California at Davis. She was gradually drawn to quiltmaking after working for several years in other areas, and has been making quilts professionally and teaching quilting classes since 1980. Her quilts have won many awards, have been published in books and magazines, and have been widely exhibited. They are in many private collections.

QUILTMAKER
Profiles

I know I speak for many other hand stitchers when I say that I prefer the quiet, timeless world that I enter as I put in stitch after stitch, establishing that intimate, tactile bond that comes from touching and caressing those fascinating pieces of colored cloth one at a time – joining them into a glorious whole.

– Cindy Vermillion Hamilton

Mary L. Hackett, a studio fiber artist living and working in Southern Illinois, has deep roots in quiltmaking and believes that innovation is the soul of quilt tradition. She has taught art to kindergarten through the sixth grade level students, and innovative techniques to people of all ages. Her work has been exhibited in quilt and art shows from coast to coast, has been published in magazines and books, and is included in private and public collections in the United States and Japan.

Jane Hall began quilting in the mid 1970s, while living in Hawaii. She is a quilt teacher, judge, and appraiser, who has co-authored four books on foundation piecing with Dixie Haywood. Her award-winning quilts have been exhibited throughout the country and are in public and private collections. Hall most often works with traditional patterns, using innovative approaches and colorations, and is especially known for her Pineapple designs.

Marilyn Henrion, a graduate of Cooper Union and a lifelong New Yorker, has been making quilts since 1975. In 1989 she retired from the faculty of The Fashion Institute of Technology to devote full time to her creative work. Her award-winning quilts have been exhibited internationally and she has had nine solo exhibitions. She has been the recipient of grants from the NY State Crafts Alliance, ArtsLink, Friends of Fiber Art International, and Nihon Vogue, and has served as vice president of Studio Art Quilt Associates.

Becky Herdle's first introduction to quilting came in 1977 when, as a 4-H leader, she took a leader training course so that she could help her club members learn about quilting. As well as being an instructor, Becky is an author, lecturer, and NQA certified judge. Her work and articles have been published in a number of books, magazines, and calendars. She has been a certified judge since 1983 and has judged at all levels. Becky has also entered her own work in shows at all levels and has received many awards.

Vickie Hallmark comments, "I make art for my sanity's sake. The creative process is a form of meditation – a way to busy the hands and mind and free the spirit to work through the serious issues of life. My quilts are therefore unsurprisingly autobiographical. Although I may have no clues as to the overriding themes during construction, in restropect the problems I was grappling with concurrently are inevitably respresented in the work. Real life solutions seem intimately connected to resolutions of artistic and technical problems during the art process."

Cindy Vermillion Hamilton (formerly Davis) began quilting while a college student in 1968. Since then she has raised three children, continues to teach seventh grade reading, and made hundreds of quilts. Born in Long Beach, CA, she has resided in Pagosa Springs, CO, since 1974. For over 30 years she has been teaching and lecturing about quilts. Her works are exhibited and published widely, and she is writing a book.

Irma Gail Hatcher began quilting in 1982 after she attended her first quilt show. Since that time, she has become nationally known for her three-dimensional hand appliqué. Hatcher teaches around the country and is the author of several books on hand appliqué. Two of her quilts have won Best Workmanship Awards at AQS shows. CONWAY ALBUM (I'M NOT FROM BALTIMORE) was also selected as one of the 100 Best American Quilts of the 20th Century.

Laura Heine took a quilting class in 1985 while expecting her first child, but is largely self-taught as a quiltmaker, specializing in machine quilting. In 1994 Heine gave up her full-time nursing position to open a quilt shop in Billings. She now teaches quilting locally and nationally, and is writing a book. In 1998 hers was one of six shops chosen to design a line of fabrics for Kings Road Fabrics. She won the challenge and continues to design for them. Her quilts are in private and corporate collections.

Ethel Hickman made two appliqué quilt tops before her marriage in 1936, and then lost interest until 1972. To improve her technique she attended workshops, studied quilt books, and subscribed to magazines. She began to compete in 1981. Her quilts have won awards and have been featured in publications. She is a member of quilt guilds and associations, has been an extension homemaker for 40 years, served on the county fair board for 37 years, and served as a 4-H leader for 10.

Chizuko Hana Hill was introduced to quilting by a friend who invited her to take a lap quilting class in 1985. Hill recalls how fortunate she felt to see the beautiful quilts at the first AQS Show and Contest while attending this class. Since that first quilting class, she has made over 25 quilts. Among these, nine were selected as finalists in the annual AQS Show and Contest, and many have won awards at the Kentucky State Fair, including Best of Show in 1995.

Mary Kay Hitchner was already an avid needleworker and dressmaker when she started quilting in 1970. She began by making small items and worked up to full-size quilts, relying on library books to teach herself the craft. By 1979, she had met others who liked to quilt and was meeting regularly with a group. Quilts are "a serious hobby" for Hitchner, who explains: "I push myself to develop or learn something new with every quilt."

Pat Holly says sewing has always been a part of her life, from sewing doll clothes as a child, to clothes for herself in high school, to costumes for shows in college. She studied weaving, fabric design, and graphic design at the University of Michigan. When her first child was born in 1983, she asked her sister for lessons and they have come to make one quilt together each year. Since 1993 Holly has also worked with Gwen Marston, illustrating six of her books.

QUILTMAKER *Profiles*

There are no simple words to describe the thrill I felt when I first walked into the Museum of the American Quilter's Society and saw my quilt on display. That one brief moment was enough to make up for its no longer being in my own collection.

– Shirley P. Kelly

Marion Huyck enrolled in a course on basic piecing in 1972 and found quiltmaking offered the perfect outlet for treasuring fabrics and using them in new ways. When she left teaching to raise her family, her quilting activity expanded. The Continental Quilting Congress launched her serious devotion. Until 1988 Huyck was a full-time quilter. Then she became a full-time teacher, and now looks forward to resuming her creative life when she retires.

Lois K. Ide became interested in quilting after winning a Stearns & Foster block contest with her Mary block. Lois has taught in the Netherlands, Nova Scotia, and the U.S. In 1988 she was awarded an Ohio Arts Council Grant; her World Peace quilt was selected by UNICEF as a greeting card for their European collection. She has been inducted into the Crawford County Senior Citizens Hall of Fame and the Ohio State Seniors Hall of Fame for sharing her quilting expertise by teaching and writing.

Vicki L. Johnson made patchwork clothing in 1969, but didn't begin quilting until 1970. Her grandmother had been an excellent seamstress, but there was not a family tradition of quilting. Johnson took a quilting class in 1970, and other workshops during the 1970s, and then began teaching. Quiltmaking is an important part of her life and she spends three to four hours in her studio daily. Her work has won awards and is included in collections, and she has authored a book.

Wilma Johnson's mother taught her the basic skills of quiltmaking. In the 1970s, shortly after she married, Johnson decided to complete three projects for Christmas. With few books available at the time, she developed her skills by learning from mistakes. She sold her baby quilts through shops, and with her sister-in-law, Carolyn Johnson, operated a mail-order business while their children were young. Now working full-time, she doesn't have time for larger quilts.

Katherine Inman began quilting because she wanted quilts she couldn't afford. In 1983 she made a cross-stitch quilt using a kit and determined she would never again make someone else's design, and hasn't. In recent years Inman has enjoyed finishing antique blocks and tops. She believes that these works into which women have put so much time deserved to be completed. In addition to quilting, Inman paints portraits and hooks rugs of her own design.

Michael James was completing his M.F.A. at the Rochester Institute of Technology when he made his first quilt. By late 1973 he had stopped painting altogether. His quilts have been featured in exhibits around the world, and are in many private and public collections. James teaches and lectures internationally, and now teaches at the University of Nebraska/Lincoln. He is author of four books, recipient of awards including three NEA fellowships, and was inducted into the Quilters' Hall of Fame in 1993.

Carolyn Johnson and her sister-in-law, Wilma Johnson, both began sewing in their teenage years. Johnson began quilting while pregnant with twins. She started with pieced quilts, then she branched out into appliqué. While their children were young, Johnson and her sister-in-law designed quilt patterns together. Working full-time now, Johnson hasn't quilted much but finds her interest is picking up again and she's becoming involved in small projects.

Melody Johnson was in her thirties when an art school classmate introduced her to quilting. She finished her first quilt in 1981, a 100" x 100" machine-pieced and hand-quilted Log Cabin. Hand quilting slowed her output, so she taught herself to machine quilt and soon began designing all original work. A professional quilt artist, Johnson travels eight months of the year, teaching around the country and operating her quilting business. Johnson comments, "When I am quilting I am supremely happy."

Angela W. Kamen initially became interested in quilting because of its combination of geometry, fabrics, and sewing. Her father had been a tailor and she liked fabrics, but wasn't interested in making clothing. When her future sister-in-law became involved in quiltmaking in the early 1970s, Kamen became interested herself. She made traditional quilts during this period, but then became involved with raising her family. In 1992 Kamen returned to quiltmaking, this time making original design work.

Margie T. Karavitis decided to make a quilted coverlet when she needed a new bedspread for a high four-poster bed. The coverlet was completed in 1972. She had always like to hand sew, but hadn't paid much attention to quilting. She says her first two projects, a cross-stitch quilt and a Diamond Star quilt, were disasters, but she continued to be interested, and her quilting improved. Karavitis especially enjoys making quilts that feature much hand quilting.

Shirley P. Kelly started making utility quilts in the mid 1980s, for family and friends. Then she visited an AQS Quilt Show and saw all that quilts could be. A high school art teacher for 33 years, she had always done drawings. When she saw quilts like Nancy S. Brown's appliqué quilts, and Charlotte Warr Andersen's THREE FOR THE CROWN, she realized that she could put animals and much more in her quilts. Kelly confesses that she despises quilting – it's the appliqué she loves.

Chris Kleppe has been quilting since the early 1980s, but adds she has always been involved with fine crafts and took "excellent fibers courses from artist Joan Paque" while completing her art degree at Mount Mary College. Kleppe finds quilting exciting "because it draws on a long folk tradition, yet leaves unlimited room for innovation." She feels her quilts use the tradition of geometric repeat patterns as a "springboard for exploration."

QUILTMAKER
Profiles

We respond to a handmade quilt, even an anonymous one, in part because through it we learn about the quilter as a homemaker, caretaker, keeper of traditions, creator of intricate patterns and symbols, and as a master craftsperson. Quilts become archetypal symbols of the women who make them.

– Jean Ray Laury

MAQS collection quilter from her preface to
Ho For California: Pioneer Women and Their Quilts

Theresa Klosterman decided in 1982 to start looking for another interest to occupy some of her time. "My youngest boy was in high school so I could see that I would soon face the empty nest syndrome. I had always liked to sew, so when I read about a quilter's guild being newly organized at the fabric store in the nearby town of Wahpeton, North Dakota, I decided to give it a try." Klosterman went to the first meeting and has been going every month since.

Susan Knight began quilting in the 1980s during a very cold winter when she wanted something to do to keep warm. Her mother and grandmother had made scrap utilitarian quilts and Knight had always been interested in crafts. She picked out a pattern in a magazine, used stretch and sew fabrics, and made a quilt. With each magazine she learned more and her skills developed. Quilting is Knight's creative outlet and she enjoys sharing her love with others.

Jean Ray Laury made her first quilt in 1956, as part of a master's degree project at Stanford University. She was making things for children, traditional in concept but contemporary in execution. Soon after, she produced enough appliqué work for her first exhibit. Laury then focused on making original design appliqué quilts, selling her designs to national women's magazines. Internationally known, Laury teaches, writes books and articles about quilting, and lectures.

Libby Lehman began quilting in 1971, as a hobby. Since then, this activity has developed into a dearly loved profession. Lehman comments, "I am a studio art quiltmaker by profession, and I work on one quilt at a time, from start to finish." Lehman teaches extensively in the U.S. and internationally. Her work is in many private, corporate, and museum collections. Her book *Thread Play* was published by That Patchwork Place, 1997.

Marzenna J. Krol, originally from Warsaw, Poland, came to the U.S. in 1981. When she was living in Lancaster Co., Pennsylvania, and working for the Mennonites, everyone had a quilting frame at home. Quilting was a part of the daily routine for people there. Krol comments, "The Mennonites' patience, understanding, and love for quilting made me understand what quilting is about."

Toni Kron decided in the late 1940s that she wanted to make a baby quilt for a niece. She asked to borrow a quilt frame from her grandmother. Her grandmother loaned her the frame, showed her how to quilt, and when the project was done gave her the frame. Kron has made quilts professionally for many years, full-time once her children were grown. Appliqué designs are her favorite; she destroys each pattern after one use "to insure that each quilt is one of a kind."

Mary E. Kuebler made her first quilt when about ten, taught by her mother. In rural Indiana, summer leisure was spent sewing quilt scraps together. Kuebler didn't quilt for years, busy assisting her husband with his service station and later selling real estate. She turned to quilting when her husband could no longer stand the click of knitting needles. She tried appliqué and then a class introduced her to the batik process she combines with quilting.

Jan Lanahan was born and raised in Australia, where she met her husband, who was serving in the U.S. Air Force. While living in Germany in the 1980s, she saw a Grandmother's Flower Garden quilt in a magazine and decided to make one. When they were later living in Phoenix, AZ, she became fascinated with Native American arts and taught herself spinning, dyeing, weaving, and coiled basketry. She continues to enjoy quilting and these other textile arts.

Lillian J. Leonard made her first quilt top, a Dresden Plate design, at the age of 11, but Leonard comments: "Quilting was not to be a ruling factor in my life until many years later." A local department store and local newspaper in Indianapolis began co-sponsoring quilt contests in the early 1980s. Leonard entered their contests held every two years. She was never among the winners until 1985, when she designed and entered a quilt that received an honorable mention.

Sharon Malec began quilting in 1992, making traditional pieced quilts. She gradually shifted to making art quilts, which are influenced by her love of animals and nature. She is most known for her realistic depictions of dogs and other animals for which she has developed her own patterns and her unique "free standing appliqué." Her work has been included in juried shows, she teaches workshops, and has recently self-published a book on her work titled *The Dog Lady Speaks*.

Marguerite Ann Malwitz has a BA degree in fine arts education and taught public school art. For many years she executed large pictorial tapestry commissions, and in 1986 began to design art quilts. Her quilts have been viewed nationally and internationally in shows, been featured in publications, and are included in public and private collections. Malwitz is committed to being a studio artist and sharing her work and life journey as a Christian artist.

Inge Mardal, Danish born, has a professional background in mechanical engineering. She has lived in Germany, USA, Canada, Denmark, France, and Belgium with her husband and son. She began quilting out of a necessity to cover a dull wall in her Paris apartment. "Fabric as a medium," comments Inge, "holds a multitude of possibilities for expressing ideas, feelings, surfaces, shapes, and invites experimentation. I continue to be fascinated by the remarkable transitions that occur between the individual phases of a project."

QUILTMAKER Profiles

I greatly enjoy employing a variety of fabrics from different sources, different eras, and different cultures. The richness they add to the quilt reflects the variety of human experience with fibers and the connections to quiltmakers of the past.

– Ruth B. McDowell

Suzanne Marshall began quilting in 1977 to make bed covers for her four children. She used scraps from making clothes and a library book on quilting. Self-taught, she has learned by trial and error. In 1989 she began entering national competitions for critiques from judges, and has since won many awards. She teaches and lectures around the country and has written a book on appliqué. A retrospective of her work in 1994 raised funds for pediatric cancer research.

Noriko Masui comments, "As a mother of two daughters, I feel happiest in my daily life, when I am designing and making quilts as an elder among them. My quilt in the MAQS collection is my present to all the people who have kindly assisted me at various quilt events." The quilt was inspired by Tibetan sand mandalas. Mandalas — graphic mystic symbols of the universe used as aids to meditation — are usually made of fabrics, but Tibetan sand mandalas are drawn on the ground with colored sands.

Mary Jo McCabe started quilting in 1979. She joined a group of 21 quilters of all levels, who each month made blocks for a different member's quilt. She didn't enjoy quiltmaking at first, but learned to. Her trip to an AQS quilt show encouraged McCabe to further develop her skills. Through the Mississippi Valley Quilters Association, she attended lectures by nationally known quilters. Her philosophy for quilting is "You'll never know if you can do it unless you try."

Marsha McCloskey made her first quilt in 1969, a scrappy quilt completely made by machine and has been working that way ever since. When the nation's bicentennial arrived, McCloskey began teaching at a shop in Seattle. Her first book was published in 1982. Since then she has written or co-authored 19 books. Specializing in the Feathered Star and other traditional designs, she has taught all over the world. She has a small publishing company and designs a line of fabric.

Jean K. Mathews began quilting in 1980. When a friend made quilted pillows one Christmas for gifts, Mathews asked for some instruction and began her own projects. Later, in going through her husband's grandmother's trunks, she found several Stearns and Foster quilt patterns and decided to make one of the quilts. A neighbor provided additional instruction and the quilt that resulted is still used by Mathews' daughter. No longer able to hand quilt because of arthritis, she enjoys machine quilting.

Laverne Mathews received B.A. and M.A. degrees from Lamar University in Beaumont, TX, and taught sixth and seventh grades in the Orange schools for 25 years. About her quiltmaking, Mathews says, "I started quilting in 1971, and have been possessed ever since, making over a hundred myself, collecting old ones, visiting museums where quilts may be seen, taking thousands of pictures, and belonging to quilt organizations." All aspects of quilting are attractive to Mathews.

Judy Mathieson, who holds a B.S. in home economics, began quilting in 1973 and teaching in 1977. She gives workshops in the U.S. and internationally. She holds NQA certification for judging and teaching. Mathieson has specialized in Mariner's Compass designs and variations, and has authored two books on the subject. She also makes quilts with dog themes as her husband trains his dogs for sheep herding and dog agility competitions.

Karin Matthiesen was inspired to begin quilting when she saw an appliqué pattern in a magazine in 1971, when she was 18. The complicated design, with its sketchy instructions, took Matthiesen years to finish. When she later moved, a nearby quilt shop offered a class and once again she was quilting. She feels her strong point in quilting is workmanship. She enjoys trying different techniques and styles, and can't imagine not quilting.

Donna Fite McConnell began quilting in 1981 when she decided to take a class with friends. McConnell was a "compulsive quilter for 18 years," owning a quilt shop, and serving on the state guild board. She has published three books, self-published patterns, been a vendor at quilt shows, and taught workshops and lectured. Physical problems have necessitated her cutting back in recent years, but she continues to edit her guild's newsletter, and enjoy her quilting friends.

Ruth B. McDowell's art education was in conjunction with the architecture department at MIT. In 1972 McDowell was inspired by Ruby McKim's *101 Patchwork Patterns* to make a set of Noon Day Lily quilts. She pieced these two quilts by machine and has continued to enjoy machine techniques. McDowell has been a full-time quiltmaker since the early 1980s. Her works are in numerous private and public collections. She teaches internationally, and is the author of five books on quiltmaking.

Keiko Miyauchi learned to sew when she was young and later went on to teach elementary school economics for three years. After Keiko's marriage and birth of her son, she began quilting after reading a quilting magazine. That was 20 years ago and Keiko continues to enjoy quiltmaking.

Barbara Pettinga Moore is an art educator, naturalist, free-lance writer, lecturer, and quiltmaker. She has a BA in art education and an MS in botany. Barbara designs all of her own art projects. These include quilts, museum exhibits, and birchbark baskets. Her quilts reflect her art/science background and her love of wildlife. The appliquéd figures in POLAR DREAMS – just finished – are adaptations of polar bear snapshots she took during a trip to Churchill, Manitoba, Canada, in 1994.

Quiltmaker *Profiles*

Mary Morgan began quilting in the 1970s when her daughters no longer wanted to wear the clothes she made. With few books and no classes available, Morgan taught herself, later learning from books as more were published. She comments, "I have a deep respect for the generations of quiltmakers who created works of beauty without the benefit of formal art training or abundant materials. I'm concerned with what my quilts do, not so much with what they say."

Laura Murray started quilting in 1989 when her daughter wanted a quilt. Murray took a course and discovered art quilts. Since then she has devoted time each year to taking workshops, and works daily in her studio. Several years ago she began to create all her own fabric. In 2000 she retired from her work in a human resource center, and has developed her professional career as an artist, teacher, and lecturer.

Julia Overton Needham had been fascinated by needlework since childhood, but didn't become seriously involved with quilting until later in life. She started a quilt when she was 13, but didn't finish it until 40 years later in 1976. The first quilt Needham entered in a competition won a blue ribbon, which spurred her on. She comments on her quiltmaking: "Quilting is only a hobby for me. I never sell my quilts. I still have them all, with the exception of the quilt in the MAQS collection."

Sue Nickels began quilting in the late 1970s, starting out by hand and gradually focusing on machine work. She has been teaching machine quilting and appliqué classes since 1990. With her sister, Pat Holly, Nickels has co-authored two books on machine quilting patterns. They also work together on quilts, including their quilt in the MAQS collection. Nickels' quilts have been featured in shows and publications. Her priorities are to make quilts using today's technology, and then share the knowledge with others.

Joyce Murrin had made utilitarian tied quilt as early as 1960, but it was in the 1970s that she became more involved in quiltmaking. She continued making bed quilts into the mid 1980s, and since 1985 has made quilts using her own original designs, each of which she uses only once. Murrin's work is exhibited throughout the United States and has been published in periodicals. She lectures and teaches, and is an active guild member and show organizer.

Claudia Clark Myers watched her grandmother run the old Singer treadle, making doll clothes, while her mother made most of her family's clothes. For 25 years Claudia designed and made costumes and now spends her retirement quilting with her daughter. "The art and craft of sewing has had a huge impact on several generations of women in my family," explains Claudia. "From doll clothes and little girls' dresses to opera headpieces and 'arty' quilts, sewing has given us all a means of self-expression, of earning respect, of earning a living."

Jan Myers-Newbury holds a B.A. from St. Olaf College and an M.A. from the University of Minnesota. Myers-Newbury is known for her geometric pieced quilts that incorporate hand-dyed fabric, most recently her shibori fabrics. She has exhibited widely and taught nationally and internationally. Nearly 200 of her works are included in corporate and private collections. Myers-Newbury began her quilting career in Minneapolis in the late 1970s, and moved to Pittsburgh in 1987.

Philippa Naylor recalls, "All I ever wanted was to be a clothes designer. And so that's what I became. After four years at college I got a job designing lingerie and by the age of 25 had become head designer." After marriage and moving to Saudi Arabia, she was introduced to quilting by a Welsh lady. Three years later, Philippa began designing her own quilts. "My hope is that the public will be attracted by the initial impact of my work and then look more closely and be inspired by the quality of the workmanship. Then I'll feel I've done my job."

Hallie H. O'Kelley had sewn since childhood, and made clothes for herself and her three daughters, but she didn't make a quilt until 1980. She had taken a screen printing class and was looking for a way to use printed fabrics. She decided to print fabrics specifically for a quilt, pieced the top, and hand quilted around the printed design, so it looked like appliqué. O'Kelley has since refined that idea, and says most of her scraps have remained unused. Quilting is an everyday part of her life.

Anne J. Oliver is a self-taught quilter who comes to quiltmaking with a good sewing background and some art training. Oliver enjoys quilt contests; she comments, "The only way I can be a quilter is to compete. It's my reason to finish!" She has already made quilts for all her family members, and loves the opportunity to express her personality through show quilts. During the years she taught, Oliver enjoyed showing frustrated quilters how to finish, stand back, look at their work, and feel good.

Betty K. Patty made her first quilt for a Grange contest in Miami County, OH, in celebration of the country's bicentennial. Patty comments: "I knew then that I had to make more. Like most grandmothers, my first thought was to make one for each of the grandchildren. After I had one for each of them I started on one for each of my sons — and it goes on and on. I can't imagine what life would be like without having a quilt in the making."

Joyce B. Peaden was taught to sew by her mother. As a young child, Peaden watched her grandmother strip piece fabrics, and later duplicated the technique. As a child she had worked with geometric shapes in games and drawing, and attributes her design abilities to this play. Peaden made her first full-size quilt in 1945. She is author of an AQS book on Irish Chain quilts, papers for the American Quilt Study Group, and many other articles on quilt history and techniques.

QUILTMAKER *Profiles*

I truly believe that as each of us breaks new ground in the advancement of the cause of quilts as art, the whole of us reaps the rewards. We can celebrate the tremendous growth in the art quilt movement and be very proud as we enter the next century.

– Yvonne Porcella
MAQS collection artist and founder of Studio Art Quilt Associates
(from *Art & Inspirations: Yvonne Porcella,* 1995)

Sylvia Pickell began "real" quilting in 1981 during her oldest daughter's senior year. She had made practice pieces and small gifts to develop the skills needed to make a special graduation gift. The quilt included fabrics from her daughter's clothes. Pickell has blocks made by her grandmother that she hopes one day to piece into a quilt. She comments, "Quilting is my creative outlet. My days are spent as a financial manager. My nights and weekends are spent with needlework of some sort."

Paul D. Pilgrim held an M.A. in jewelry design and taught art and art history to junior high students. He learned basic sewing as a child, but it was the discovery of his grandmother's unfinished quilt tops in the mid 1970s that involved him with quiltmaking. As he and partner Gerald E. Roy bought antiques for their antiques shops and their own folk art collections, Pilgrim also collected quilt blocks and scraps from the past for his quilts. He was an accomplished quiltmaker, teacher, and appraiser.

Sharon Rauba began quilting in around 1980; she was tired of making clothes that never fit and thought that would not be a concern with quilts. She read library books, joined a quilt group, and began trying different techniques. She found she really liked appliqué. As she worked with designs she reached a point where she wanted to design her own, and has been doing that ever since. She continues to quilt, but also enjoys many other interests like gardening and needlepoint.

Wendy M. Richardson can't remember a time when she didn't sew. She recalls trying to be helpful as her mother and grandmother worked with a variety of needle arts. Richardson became interested in quilting in 1975, when she took a leave of absence for the birth of her son. She has been quilting ever since and belongs to several quilt groups. She comments, "The great support of a quilt group and the learning experience has helped me immeasurably."

Yvonne Porcella, an artist specializing in wearable art and art quilts, began in 1962 making unique garments and woven wallhangings. In 1980 she exhibited her first art quilts. Her work has toured in national and international shows, and is collected by individuals, corporations, and museums. Porcella teaches and lectures in the United States and abroad, is the author of eight books, and was the founder of Studio Art Quilt Associates. In 1998 she was inducted into the Quilters' Hall of Fame.

Fay Pritts appliquéd her first quilt top in 1974, which was quilted by her grandmother, who quilted people's tops professionally. Pritts made other quilt tops and embroidered, but she didn't quilt any until 1983. After her grandmother's death she discovered a box of her Friendship blocks. Pritts decided to stitch them together and quilt them. She and her husband now make quilts professionally, and it is Fay who does all the quilting. Once she tried hand quilting, she found she liked it.

Julee Prose's interest in quilting began in 1974. Her first quilt was a six-point (rather than eight-point) Lone Star because she drafted the pattern incorrectly. Her grandmother had showed her how to quilt but she was otherwise self-taught. In the 1980s she operated a mail-order business, designing wall quilts and small pieces for hoops. Prose enjoys quilt competitions; they encourage her to pay attention to every detail. She especially likes doing hand quilting.

Doris Amiss Rabey began quilting in 1973 when she inherited two tops she wanted to finish. She joined the National Quilting Association to learn, won a ribbon in her first show, and has been making quilts ever since then. Many of her quilts have won awards or have appeared in publications. Rabey comments: "For each quilt, wallhanging, or block I make, I find a new technique to try. This is what keeps quilting so interesting, satisfying, and fulfilling. I only wish I had started quilting sooner."

Lucretia Romey spends several months at sea each year teaching painting and drawing. She accompanies her husband, who lectures on oceanography. Her wall quilts are a result of drawings done in her yard or while traveling. Romey began quilting in the 1970s, while living in Boulder, CO. She had been painting watercolors, but decided to sew a landscape rather than painting it. Ever since her studio has been half for painting and half for quilting.

Solveig Ronnqvist says it was a book by Jean Ray Laury that in the mid 1970s inspired her to take a quilting class. She was soon hooked. Ronnqvist had grown up in Finland, where sewing, crocheting, and knitting were very much a part of everyday life, and in the United States she had completed a degree in fashion design and merchandising. After making several traditional pieces, Ronnqvist soon realized she wanted to make smaller, original design quilts. Ronnqvist has a studio and sews all the time.

Lonni Rossi first encountered surface design and quilting while majoring in advertising and graphic design at Moore College of Art & Design in Philadelphia. Involved in her graphic design career, she didn't return to quilting until after the birth of her son in 1987. Since then she has become increasingly involved with quilting, which now shares equal billing with her fabric painting business and graphic design activities. With two other art quilters, Rossi has recently formed Studio Three.

Adrien Rothschild was born in Baltimore and exhibited her paintings and photographs locally in the 1970s. She received a B.A. in biology from The Johns Hopkins University and in 1978 began her first quilt, solely for practical use. After several years of working as a bicycle mechanic, she turned to quiltmaking full time in 1985. Her works have appeared in many shows, have won awards, and regularly appear in periodicals. Her quilts are also in private and corporate collections.

QUILTMAKER
Profiles

I consider my greatest achievement
as having kept my family's quilting tradition alive at a
time when domestic skills
were not taught, acknowledged, or respected.
It is only now that the cultural, historical,
and artistic value of American
women's quiltmaking is being recognized.

– Lyn Peare Sandberg

Gerald E. Roy comes to quiltmaking from a fine arts background. After receiving an MFA in painting, he taught art for 10 years in Oakland, California. Growing up in Massachusetts, he developed a deep love and appreciation for American antiques. He is the curator of the famed Pilgrim/Roy Collection, one of the finest collections of antique quilts in America. As a quiltmaker, he has always look at quilts as "art," rather than just decoration or utility, looking to capture tradition as well as craft.

Linda M. Roy's passion is designing traditional quilts using mostly handwork techniques. Raised in Massachusetts, she was introduced to quiltmaking in 1989. Having no formal art background, Roy delights in working with color and simple techniques. Projects can begin in different ways — sometimes it's a piece of fabric and sometimes it's visualization of a complete arrangement. Roy frequently preassembles components such as ruching and bias bars to support her appliqué arrangements.

Elsie Schlabach designed her first quilt in 1957, a crib quilt for her first child, and continued to make quilts for her family of four children. Later, Schlabach started to make Amish quilt reproductions. She comments, "I have discovered that color is the most important element in successfully re-creating Amish quilts. It is possible to come very close to the old look if careful attention is given to fabric selection, pattern scale, and quilting design."

Cynthia Schmitz began concentrating on building her skills in machine quilting so she could produce the extensive quilting designs that she loved in Amish and Provencal quilts. The first two quilts she entered in national competitions won awards. She describes her art form as a "combination of everything she loves: color, fabric, sewing, and problem solving."

Margaret Rudd grew up in rural Kentucky, where quilting was something women did. She completed several tops while a teenager, using scraps from dresses and carding cotton for the filler. Rudd then taught school, worked as a home economist, and later returned to the Trigg County School system filling several administrative roles. In 1983 she joined a newly formed quilt guild and returned to quilting. Recently, Rudd has shared her skills with young people at school and in her home.

Linda Karel Sage began quilting in 1980, while living in Chicago. She was running a small gallery and printmaking studio and had met two quilters who inspired her to mount an exhibit of art quilts. Gradually Sage moved from printmaking to quiltmaking as her primary medium. She was excited by the prospect of working in color. New ideas seemed to be five years ahead of her ability to produce the work, so she tried to develop techniques that allowed her to work much faster.

Lyn Peare Sandberg began hand piecing Grandmother's Flower Garden blocks with an aunt in 1960. Two of her aunts were prolific makers of practical quilts. From 1975 through 1995 Sandberg was a professional quiltmaker, hand quilting vintage tops for families, restoring and repairing quilts, and completing original-design commissioned quilts. In 1995 Sandberg began creating mosaics from vintage pottery. Since then quilting has become a hobby, but it remains integral to her life.

Rose Sanders became interested in quilts after she bought an old rope bed and decided that she wanted an authentic bedcover for it — preferably a quilt. When she started quilting, she had no idea what she was getting into since the only other needlework she had done was crewel embroidery. She has now gone on to make more quilts, but comments: "I truly believe in quality, not quantity." Rose always devotes whatever length of time is necessary to ensure that her quilts receive the meticulous care they deserve.

Elaine M. Seaman's first quilt was a 1972 attempt made of sewing remnants from 4-H projects. "It radiated enthusiasm, if not skill," she notes. When she moved to Kalamazoo in 1978, she and like-minded women formed the Log Cabin Quilters, a group still going strong today. She taught quiltmaking for 15 years and still quilts, although more as a hobby than an obsession now. She comments: "I love it when an idea strikes me and I can cut, cut, cut."

Judy Seidel learned to make a quilted pillow in a fabric store class and she's been quilting ever since. She had sewed her own clothes for years but hadn't quilted. After teaching kindergarten all day, she enjoys having some hand quilting or other needlework for the evenings. Designing quilts, machine stitching borders, and other less relaxing activities are saved for weekends. Seidel "thrives on handwork some might find tedious." New doors to quilting will open as she's retiring in June 2001.

Audree L. Sells came from a family of quilters, but didn't make her first serious quilt until 1986, after 35 years of teaching elementary school and painting as a hobby. She was inspired by a Baltimore Album style quilt on display at the Minnesota Quilters Show. Sells enjoys developing new techniques and sharing them through lectures, workshops, exhibits, and articles.

Polly Sepulvado, M.D., has been quilting since 1975. She quilts every day and has had a quilt frame in her den for hand quilting since 1976. Always learning new techniques has fueled Sepulvado's passion for quilting. She's recently begun to incorporate machine embroidery using a machine her husband gave her. She displays her quilts on beds in her home and in her office, rotating them every few months so returning patients see different quilts.

QUILTMAKER Profiles

I make quilts that are meant to be used, loved, enjoyed, shared, washed, and yes, worn out. I grew up where lots of people quilted – it was part of what they did.

– Martha B. Skelton

Jonathan Shannon, the first male winner of the AQS Best of Show Award, hopes that his award will encourage other men to enter the quilt world. Shannon began quilting in 1989 when he wanted to make a bed quilt. With no tradition of quilting in his family or friends who quilted, he took many classes his first two years. For several years Shannon was very active in quiltmaking, but in recent years quiltmaking has played a secondary role to other interests.

Marion Shenk began quiltmaking in 1940 at the age of nine. She watched her mother, aunts, and grandmother at their regular quilting bees held all winter long in each others' homes. Shenk wanted to learn – it looked like fun. While growing up, she knew of no bedspreads other than quilts. Her mother taught her to quilt and the quilts and blocks she has since made have won awards. Shenk designs projects for House of White Birches publishing.

Nancy Ann Sobel comments "My mother died when I was three years old, but God gave me a wonderful country grandmother who spent quality time teaching me to use a needle and thread." Sobel darned her first sock at age four, learned to use a treadle sewing machine at age seven, and started her first quilt top when about 12, slowly working on appliqué blocks for several years. Sobel quilts as often as she can, but says her garden "can get in the way."

Judy Sogn began quilting in 1982, to make gifts for family members for whom she couldn't sew clothes. There was no family tradition of quilting, but quiltmaking has become central to Sogn's life: "I think about quilts every day, even when I am not actually working on a project." Her quilts have won awards, and Sogn says she plans much of her life around quilting, taking handwork for visits with family and friends, and making trips that include quilt shows.

Judy Simmons, author of two books on textile arts, muses, "I probably should have been suspicious when at the age of five I was more intrigued by my mother's box of scraps than anything else." A former home economics teacher, Simmons has been sewing for as long as she can remember. She especially enjoys art quilts and appliqué. With her current busy schedule, she completes everything by machine. Simmons creates all the fabrics for her quilts.

Martha B. Skelton grew up in a family where everyone quilted, and was soon hand sewing herself. She made a Six Point Star scrap quilt and has loved that type of quilt since. Skelton completed a BA in geology and an MA in library science from the University of Oklahoma, married, and continued to quilt. She organized several quilting groups and helped start a state organization. Skelton has encouraged many others to quilt by teaching classes throughout Mississippi, her home state since 1947.

Ruth Britton Smalley says that various forms of art have always been a source of pleasure for her, and that painting, sculpture, and jewelry making led her to the art of making quilts. Her quilting experience began around 1983, while she was working in a quilt shop. Though she holds a B.A. in art and interior design, she feels she has much to learn in the areas of quilt construction techniques. She adds: "Using fabrics instead of paint, and scissors instead of drawing has involved great pleasure and revelation."

Lois T. Smith began quiltmaking with a passion in 1980. She had previously made a baby quilt by hand for her son in 1956, but become consumed with the demands of a large family. In 1979 Smith began making art pieces while working for Stretch-and-Sew, was invited to teach quiltmaking, and thus developed her interest. She now teaches internationally and has authored two books on machine quiltmaking. Smith draws energy from her quiltmaking and quilts nearly every day.

Patricia Spadaro became interested in quilting in the early 1980s because of a neighbor. This friend taught a class on hand piecing and hand quilting. Spadaro is the only student from the class who is still quilting. She had never quilted as a child, but she had sewed clothing, draping clothes and making suits for herself. She had worked with Simplicity Patterns as well. Spadaro continues to like traditional patterns and quilts, and enjoys hand quilting. She is especially fond of making whole-cloth quilts.

Doreen Speckmann began quiltmaking in 1977 after many years as an expert knitter, needlepointer, and spinner. She became internationally known for her innovative adaptations of traditional patterns and her use of Peaky and Spike shapes to create the illusion of curves from straight piecing. Her work has been displayed extensively, she wrote two books, and taught workshops world-wide, generously sharing her skills and her humor, especially on quilting cruises.

Louise Stafford (right) and her twin sister were born in 1909 on the Becker farm in Kansas, where quilting was one of the many "chores." At an early age their mother had them cut cloth scraps into patches and place them in a shoebox. Stafford explains, "When a box became full, a quilt would be put together by hand or by treadle sewing machine. Quilting was work to us then, but now it is my recreation and pleasure." Stafford continues to make quilts and play golf weekly.

Aileen Stannis, a retired nurse, has been quilting for 25 years. In 1991 she learned the appliqué needle-turn technique from Elly Sienkiewicz and that's when her quiltmaking really "took off." Stannis always works on several quilts at a time, and always feels a great sense of accomplishment with each finished quilt. Stannis appreciates machine work but enjoys doing everything by hand herself.

QUILTMAKER
Profiles

Quiltmaking has given me a sense of self, of achievement, of self esteem. Sharing Baltimore appliqué techniques, watching others flourish, has filled me with such positive feelings.

– Sherry Sunday

Arlene Statz feels she is not an artist, so she prefers to "stick to the more traditional patterns." She explains about her quilting that being a farmer's wife, her quilting time is September through April. She has five grown children and most of her quilts are passed on to them and her grandchildren. Now retired, Statz continues to quilt, though travels with her husband leave less time for quiltmaking. She continues to attend classes and participates in her local guild.

Carole Steiner has always loved quilts. Even as a child she had admired one on a girlfriend's bed. After her husband retired, they moved and she discovered her new next door neighbor was a quilter. Soon Steiner was making hand-pieced quilts herself, using cereal box templates. Since then, quilting has been an important part of her life. Steiner especially enjoys the handwork and the way the quilting brings many diverse women together to create a sisterhood.

Janice Streeter began quilting in 1977. Her mother had been an avid quilter, but had not shared her skills, so Streeter developed her own style. She speaks of herself as "a conformist" but says quilting seems to be her "way of breaking the rules and expressing individuality." Streeter quilts with both hands on top of the quilt, makes one stitch at a time, makes her own thimbles, does not use a quilting needle, and uses her quilting hoop backwards.

Karmen Streng began sewing before junior high school and her original college major was in the home economics field, though she finished with a masters in social work. She took her first quilting class in 1976, after retiring from a career as a social worker, and became hooked on quilting. She became involved in competitions and won awards. In 1986 Streng developed a physical condition that has prevented her from doing handwork, but she continues to enjoy making bed pieces for fun.

Joyce Stewart began quiltmaking when she was asked to piece a quilt for her church group in 1981. Using a book of quilt patterns, she made a Rolling Star quilt top, but didn't fall in love with quilting until 1982 when she saw a strip-pieced Lone Star quilt in a quilt shop and signed up for a class. Soon she and her sister Ann Seely were making a quilt together and they have both been quilting ever since. She and her sister have co-authored two books and teach nationally.

Frances Stone learned to quilt at the age of nine, when her mother involved her in making a Nine-Patch quilt top. Stone enjoyed making the top, but didn't quilt again until an accident left her in a full cast for about nine weeks. She purchased a cross stitch quilt kit and by the time she was done, she was hooked. She returned to full-time work, but continued to collect books and make an occasional quilt. In the early 1960s her quiltmaking activities increased. Stone now makes mostly baby quilts.

Elaine Stonebraker made her first quilt "quite by accident" in 1981, needing a project that didn't cost any money. Deciding she liked it, she took classes and read books. Never happy with a repetitive project, she developed a method for creating pictorial pieced quilts. Stonebraker comments, "Quilting has changed my life, giving me a dimension that sewing clothing never did." She continues to always have a project on her design board.

Dorothy Mackley Stovall explains that quiltmaking was not a part of her heritage. In 1972 she retired after 30 years of nursing, and her husband began talking of a new house. She decided to make a quilt for it. Two years later she made a second one, and in 1978 "discovered the wonderful world of quilting – classes, guilds, publications, shows, workshops, and contests." Stovall adds, "I decided I would strive for quality rather than quantity, and piece and quilt by hand."

Marie Sturmer's formal art training began at the Cranbrook Art Academy. She earned a secondary teaching degree in art education from Alma College and an M.F.A. degree from Wayne University. Years of classroom activities with art students reinforced her ability to adapt many artistic skills and techniques. The stencil-painted quilts of the 1820s fascinate her and have dominated her quilting ventures. Sturmer comments, "I take great pride in extending this American style of quiltmaking to the 2000s."

Eileen Bahring Sullivan retired from teaching in 1972 to raise a family and pursue her own art. She became involved in quiltmaking "innocently and very traditionally" in the late 1970s and began entering juried competitions with the first AQS show in 1985. Though largely self-taught, she has taken workshops in special techniques and now teaches workshops herself, and self publishes patterns. Sullivan strives for both artistic and technical excellence.

Sherry Sunday began quilting in the early 1970s, embroidering blocks on linen. When her children came along Sunday had less time, but kept noticing quilts in publications and dreamed of making them. In 1977 the Sundays purchased a Victorian home, and by 1978 she was making quilts for the beds using two books she had purchased. By the mid 1980s she was teaching in many shops, and soon opened her own shop for a while. In the early 1990s she began teaching nationally.

Gabrielle Swain is best known for her use of color and her craftsmanship. She is a self-confused theatre rat who took up quilting in 1983. Ranging from realistic to abstract, her work explores man and his relationship to nature. Gabrielle is one of the founding members of North Texas Quilt Artists.

Quiltmaker *Profiles*

*O*ne day I was watching a TV interview
with a singer. When the interviewer asked her
if a comeback was worth the uphill struggle,
she answered, "I can't NOT sing."
Turning to my husband, I said, "That's it! I can't NOT
quilt. It's part of who I am."

– Elsie Vredenburg

Myrl Lehman Tapungot worked with ten other quilters for seven months to complete her quilt in the MAQS collection. Tapungot began seriously quilting in 1984. She had always loved fiber arts, especially quilting. A friend who was also a teacher helped Tapungot become a professional quilter.

Deborah Warren Techentin says of her interest in quilting, "Since early childhood I have been fascinated by making things with needle and thread." For many years this interest was channeled into home sewing and needlework; nothing was bought that could be made. In 1982 I took a quilting class, and I was hooked.

Marjorie D. Townsend was reared in Trousdale and Macon Counties, TN, where quilting was a family tradition. Townsend comments, "I learned the fundamentals of quilting at an early age, but didn't begin quilting as an art until the early 1980s." Townsend made several cross-stitch quilts, and then learned to hand quilt them in a class with Mildred Locke. Townsend has quilted for years, especially during the winter months. For her, quilting is a release, like playing golf. You can forget anything else.

Trigg County Quilters are a group of about 70 quilters living in the Barkley Lake (KY & TN) area. Established in 1983, they meet regularly and are very involved in community service, coordinating a quilt show and community displays, contributing books to their library, contributing to the school's scholarship fund, and sponsoring a quilting club there as well. When MAQS was founded in 1991, 100% of the guild's members became MAQS friends, and they volunteer monthly at MAQS.

Barbara Temple was encouraged to begin quilting by her Coral Springs, FL, neighbor Judy Simmons. From the start, she was interested in making original design picture quilts. Temple continues to enjoy the design process – the challenge of creating a picture with depth and dimension. She enjoys making a quilt like a painting. Currently work and a new granddaughter keep Temple from quilting, but she hopes to return to it. She encourages even those who have no experience with handwork to try quilting.

Joyce Ann Tennery says a needle and thread were familiar tools for her, as she learned sewing skills from her mother. An NQA certified judge, in the 1980s quiltmaking became a full-time career for Tennery. With a degree in education, it was a natural transition for her to begin teaching quiltmaking in the early 1980s. Tennery feels that with her work, she carries on the tradition, exploring design and color with each new work.

Leureta Beam Thieme, the oldest of five children, began sewing at the age of ten, making clothes for herself and her younger sisters. She began quilting in 1970 when friends encouraged her to join them in making special projects. Thieme has made many quilts and taught hand quilting at a local college. Having started her own business designing original clothing, Thieme doesn't have much time to quilt, but looks forward to returning to the art in the future.

Judith Thompson has been seriously quilting since 1983. With no one in her immediate family to learn from, she is largely self-taught. Quilting has become the focus of her life, with several works always in progress and several quilts in shows or traveling exhibits. She teaches locally, but likes to keep time free to create her own work. She is inspired by antique quilts and tries to use ideas from them for her own work. Her quilts have won many awards.

Ludmila Uspenskaya has been working in textiles since graduating from the Mukhina Art School in St. Petersburg, Russia, in 1967. For an exhibit that year, she originated the "fabric collage," technique she still uses. She began quilting in 1989 when invited to submit a quilt for an exhibit at the All Russia Museum of Decorative, Applied, and Folk Art. Inspired by nature, Ludmila works full-size in fabric from the beginning. She moved to New York, New York, in 1994.

Elsie Vredenburg's grandmother involved her in quilting when she was 17, but Vredenburg had been sewing since 13 and had always slept under quilts and been fascinated by them. For years she made her children's clothing. When they were grown, she returned to quilting, spurred by the 1976 Bicentennial.

Carol Ann Wadley started quilting in the 1960s when she had three small children, an Air Force career pilot husband, a lot of scraps from pajamas and play clothes, and a few spare moments. She has continued to make quilts over the years, still doing her own hand quilting, but now piecing them by machine. Most of her quilts were bed size. By the 1980s Wadley had begun creating her own original designs. She almost always starts a new quilt on New Year's Day.

Debra Wagner began quilting in the 1970s, to teach piecing classes in her family's fabric and sewing machine store. A clothing and textile design major, she had learned the craft in college. Wagner had also been creating award-winning machine embroidery for over 10 years. She later took a machine quilting class from Harriet Hargrave and went on from there. Wagner no longer pursues quilting as a career, but continues to enjoy making quilts as a hobby.

QUILTMAKER
Profiles

If I didn't have anything else to do I would just sew. I've always liked working with color. When I was a little girl my momma would be sewing and throw scraps on the floor. I would get them and play with the colors.

– Anna Williams

Deborah Lynn Ward's sister-in-law, Moneca Calvert comments, "Though a quilter fewer then five years, Debbie had created an impressive body of work considering she was the mother of young children. She had developed machine appliqué and machine quilting techniques and won local competitions at least three of those five years. Her death in 1991 was untimely in every possible way." Her piece in the MAQS collection represents her signature style.

Anna Williams watched her mother and grandmother make quilts. She would "pick up the strings of materials that fell to the floor" and make doll dresses. At nine, she recalls making a baby quilt. Born on a plantation near Baton Rouge, Williams attended the plantation school and worked in the fields. Her family later moved to town, where she worked as a domestic. Now that her eight children are grown, Williams has more time to make quilt tops. Included in many collections, her work is nationally known.

Marlene Brown Woodfield began quilting in 1976, to make a gift for her daughter's graduation from high school. Woodfield had sewn in 4-H and used these skills to complete a twin size quilt for her daughter's dorm bed. Woodfield's second quilt was made in 1980 when her daughter again graduated. By this time classes were available, so she took classes, and soon discovered she most liked appliquéing her own original designs. Now retired from pre-school teaching, she quilts daily.

Juanita Gibson Yeager was inspired to explore quiltmaking after seeing a Georgia Bonesteel PBS-TV quilting segment in 1983. At the time Yeager was working full time as a registered nurse. She taught herself, using books, and then enrolled in an adult education class. Over the next years she studied with national instructors, and in 1991 left nursing to make quilts full time. She belongs to a quilt/fiber artist group, teaches regionally, and exhibits and sells her work nationally.

QUILTMAKER
Awards

Beverly Mannisto Williams, tired of making "disposable" projects, turned to quilting for something more lasting. In the 1980s she worked with a group that met to help each other with quilting projects. Williams had sewn clothes for her boys, and used her basic skills to make a simple pieced Maple Leaf quilt. Then she made a small whole-cloth quilt and discovered she loved hand quilting. She's currently involved with family as a caregiver, but looks forward to quilting more in the future.

Cassandra Williams is a former oil painter, who switched mediums into the world of quilts. She uses a number of techniques to perfect her quilts—both machine and handwork. In the making of THE MAP MAKERS, Williams utilized raw edge appliqué, machine free-motion quilting, paint, and beading to portray Lewis, Clark, and Sacajawea on the trail west. In the bottom panel of the quilt, Fort Clatsop and dwellings along the trail are represented. All details are authentic according to the artist's historical research.

Louise Young started quilting in 1972, with a quilt entitled WATERGATE WONDER. She liked sewing, but was tired of making clothes that never fit. Quilts would not have to fit anything. Young learned by trial and error, and became interested in needlework by other cultures. She now takes needlework groups on tours of the San Blas Islands. Young has a master's degree in botany, and most of her quilts are based on the plant world. She quilts nearly every day.

Nadene Zowada was taught to quilt by her mother and her grandmother who she helped with hand piecing. She started her first large quilt in the 1950s, a Postage Stamp bed quilt that included materials gathered from various states she and her husband had visited that summer. Zowada comments, "My husband and I lived for 30 years high in the Big Horn Mountains. The long winters provided many hours for crafts. I enjoy many types of crafts, creative stitchery, sewing, as well as quilting."

A number of quiltmakers represented in the MAQS Founders Collection have received national awards for their work, in some cases for the very quilts in the collection.

Central to the MAQS collection are the winners of the purchase awards at the AQS Quilt Show & Contest, held annually since 1985 in Paducah, Kentucky. The Best of Show, Hand Workmanship, Machine Workmanship, and Best Wall Quilt awards in this show are all purchase awards. Listed on pages 134 and 135 are Founders Collection quilts that are in the collection because they have been the recipients of these prestigious awards.

Also recognized on these pages are the 22 Founders Collection artists whose quilts were designated as being among the 100 Best American Quilts of the Twentieth Century. Seven of the specific quilts selected are included in the MAQS Collection.

The MAQS Founders Collection also includes nine quiltmakers who have made pieces designated by the National Quilting Association as Masterpiece Quilts, which makes these individuals members of the Master's Guild. Six of the quilts that earned these quiltmakers this distinction are included in the MAQS Founders Collection.

Among the collection quiltmakers are award winners in Quilt National, the biennial juried art quilt competition and exhibit.

These are only a selection of the many awards that have been won by quiltmakers represented in the MAQS Founders Collection. Many of the quiltmakers have won awards at the local, state, or national level.

100 BEST AWARDS

In preparation for a special exhibit held in Houston, Texas, October 20–24, 1999, at the International Quilt Festival, 100 quilts were selected as the top American quilts in the twentieth century. Seven of those selected through what has been called "The Ultimate Quilt Search" are in the MAQS Founders Collection.

These quilts were chosen by a panel of distinguished experts. Twenty-nine panelists nominated over 1,700 quilts made between 1900 and 1999, and then painstakingly whittled that list down. Seven quilts in the MAQS collection were among those selected, and 22 quiltmakers in the collection were represented.

Artists in the MAQS collection chosen as having made a quilt among the Century's 100 Best American Quilts are:

Charlotte Warr Andersen

Faye Anderson

Jane Blair
    GYPSY IN MY SOUL, page 71

Moneca Calvert

Chris Wolf Edmonds

Caryl Bryer Fallert
    CORONA II: SOLAR ECLIPSE, page 77

Candy Goff
    JOIE DE VIE – JOY OF LIFE, page 63

Alison Goss
    ANCIENT DIRECTIONS, page 77

Irma Gail Hatcher
    CONWAY ALBUM (I'M NOT FROM BALTIMORE),
    page 39

Michael James

Shirley P. Kelly

Jean Ray Laury

Libby Lehman

Susan Marshall
    TOUJOURS NOUVEAU, page 45

Judy Mathieson

Ruth B. McDowell

Jan Myers-Newbury

Anne J. Oliver

Yvonne Porcella

Jonathan Shannon
    AIR SHOW, page 15

Debra Wagner

Beverly Mannisto Williams

AQS QUILT SHOW
Awards

BEST OF SHOW AWARD/AQS QUILT SHOW
Sponsored by AQS 1985 – 1998
Sponsored by Hancock's of Paducah 1999 – 2004

1985 – Oriental Fantasy by Katherine Inman, page 32
1986 – Spring Winds by Faye Anderson, page 31
1987 – Autumn Radiance by Sharon Rauba, page 37
1988 – Gypsy in My Soul by Jane Blair, page 71
1989 – Corona II: Solar Eclipse by Caryl Bryer Fallert, page 77
1990 – The Beginnings by Dawn Amos, page 72
1991 – Dawn Splendor by Nancy Ann Sobel, page 22
1992 – Momma's Garden by Anne J. Oliver, page 31
1993 – Air Show by Jonathan Shannon, page 15
1994 – Wild Rose by Fay Pritts, page 38
1995 – Migration #2 by Caryl Bryer Fallert, page 93
1997 – Vintage Rose Garden by Judith Thompson, page 35
1998 – The Beatles Quilt by Pat Nickels and Sue Holly, page 82
1999 – Joie de Vie – Joy of Life by Candy Goff, page 63
2000 – Birds of a Different Color by Caryl Bryer Fallert, page 50
2001 – Kells: Magnum Opus by Zena Thorpe
2002 – Welcome to My Dreams by Betty Ekern Suiter
2003 – Lime Light by Philippa Naylor, page 101
2004 – Spice of Life by Linda M. Roy, page 103

HAND WORKMANSHIP AWARD/AQS QUILT SHOW
Sponsored by Gingher Inc. 1985 – 1998
Sponsored by Timeless Treasures 1999 – 2002

1985 – Dot's Vintage 1983 by Dorothy Finley, page 62
1986 – Bed of Peonies by Karin Matthieson, page 65
1987 – Victorian Fantasy of Feathers and Lace by Beverly Mannisto Williams, page 69
1989 – Spring Flower Baskets by Janice Streeter, page 70
1990 – Midwinter Night's Dream by Nancy Ann Sobel, page 60
1991 – Tennessee Pink Marble by Julia Overton Needham, page 65
1992 – Mystery by Claudia Edmonds
1993 – Toujours Nouveau by Suzanne Marshall, page 45
1994 – Conway Album (I'm Not from Baltimore) by Irma Gail Hatcher, page 39
1995 – Lilies Are Forever by Carole Steiner, page 66

1996—Baltimore Remembered by Aileen Stannis, page 34

1997—Le Jardin de Nos Reves by Myrl Lehman Tapungot and friends, page 67

2000—Garden Maze by Irma Gail Hatcher, page 19

2001—Blue Earth Filled with Water and Flowers by Keiko Miyauchi, page 98

2002—Mother's Day by Suzanne Marshall, page 100

2003—Star Flower by Elsie M. Campbell, page 102

2004—Victorian Elegance by Jane E. Holihan

MACHINE WORKMANSHIP AWARD/AQS QUILT SHOW
Sponsored by Bernina of America, Inc., 1993 – 2004

1993—Floral Urns by Debra Wagner, page 81

1994—One Fish, Two Fish, Red Fish, Blue Fish by Laura Heine, page 82

1995—Sunburst Quilt by Debra Wagner, page 46

1996—Goato and Friends by Barbara Barber, page 79

1997—Kettle Moraine Star by Diane Gaudynski, page 78

1998—Sweetheart on Parade by Diane Gaudynski, page 81

1999—Butternut Summer by Diane Gaudynski, page 80

2000—October Morning by Diane Gaudynski, page 80

2001—Enlightenment by Vickie Hallmark, page 98

2002—Pop Stars by Philippa Naylor, page 99

2003—Blueberry Morning by Cynthia Schmitz, page 101

2004—The Space Quilt by Sue Nickels & Pat Holly, page 103

BEST WALL QUILT AWARD/AQS QUILT SHOW
Sponsored by RJR Fashion Fabrics, 1989 – 2004

1989—Looking Back on Broken Promises by Dawn Amos, page 26

1990—Tulips Aglow by Mary Kay Hitchner, page 50

1991—Ancient Directions by Alison Goss, page 77

1992—Descending Visions by Dawn Amos, page 40

1993—Mount Pleasant Miners by Nancy S. Brown, page 28

1994—Hammered at Home by Iris Aycock, page 78

1995—Hot Fun by Melody Johnson, page 76

1996—Raggedy Sun Worshippers by Jane Blair, page 18

1997—Heliacal Rise by Laura Murray, page 79

1998—Jelly Bean by Angela W. Kamen, page 87

1999—Cabins in the Cosmos by Lonni Rossi, page 94

2000—…And Friends of the Family by Shirley P. Kelly

2001—It's Not Summer Yet by Inge Mardal, page 100

2002—Who's Your Poppy? by Claudia Clark Myers, page 99

2003—Totem by Gabrielle Swain, page 102

2004—Sun-Bathing Blue Tit by Inge Mardal, page 103

MASTERPIECE QUILT AWARDS

The Master's Guild, comprised of makers of masterpiece quilts, was created in 1980 by the National Quilting Association (NQA) "as a way to award formal recognition for a high degree of excellence in the design and execution of quiltmaking." Membership in the Master's Guild is the highest award NQA bestows on a quiltmaker. Quilts nominated for consideration or submitted by their makers are evaluated by NQA certified judges. Quilts that receive this honor have to be nearly perfect in workmanship and also have outstanding design.

Dorothy Finley, 1983
    DOT'S VINTAGE 1983, page 62

Caryl Bryer Fallert, 1986

Julia Needham, 1986

Beverly Mannisto Williams, 1987
    VICTORIAN FANTASY OF FEATHERS & LACE, page 69

Linda Goodmon Emery, 1987
    ROSEMALING INSPIRATION, page 31

Rose Sanders, 1987
    CROWN OF CERISE, page 33

Janice Streeter, 1990
    SPRING FLOWER BASKETS, page 70

Debra Wagner, 1992

Irma Gail Hatcher, 1995
    CONWAY ALBUM (I'M NOT FROM BALTIMORE), page 39

QUILT NATIONAL AWARDS

Quilt National is a biennial international juried competition of contemporary innovative quilts. Initially organized by Nancy Crow, Francoise Barnes, Virginia Randles, and a dedicated corps of volunteers, since 1979, Quilt National has showcased exciting and innovative trends in the medium.

Quiltmakers in the Founders Collection who have served as jurors include: Michael James (1979), Jan Myers-Newbury (1987), Chris Wolf Edmonds (1989), Yvonne Porcella (1989), Judi Warren Blaydon (1993), Libby Lehman (1995), and Caryl Bryer Fallert (1999).

•BEST OF SHOW AWARD
    Jan Myers-Newbury, 1993

•DOMINI McCARTHY MEMORIAL AWARD FOR EXCELLENCE IN CRAFTSMANSHIP
    Judy Mathieson, 1987

•TRAILBLAZER AWARD
    Faye Anderson, 1999

•PEOPLE'S CHOICE AWARD
    B. J. Elvgren, 1983
        TWELVE DAYS OF CHRISTMAS, page 33
    Judy Mathieson, 1987
    Ruth B. McDowell, 1989

QUILT SOURCES

DONATED TO MAQS BY INDIVIDUALS & ORGANIZATIONS

Amish Easter Baskets, donated by Elsie Vredenburg; Barking Up the Wrong Tree, donated by Meredith Schroeder; Celebration of Autumn, donated by Karmen Streng; Cherry Rose, donated by Margie Karavitis; Designer Christmas Trees, donated by Adrien Rothschild; Dresden Garden, donated by Gerald E. Roy; Great American Elk, donated by Chizuko Hana Hill; Indian Barn Raising, donated by Becky Herdle; Javanese Jungle, donated by Audree L. Sells; A Mandala of Flowers, donated by Noriko Masui; Morning Glory, donated by Mary Chartier; Mt. St Helens, Did You Tremble? donated by Joyce Peaden; Night Flowers, donated by Moneca Calvert; Oh My Stars, donated by Margie Karavitis; Olde English Medallion, donated by Cindy Vermillion-Hamilton; Poppies & Other California Beauties, donated by Canyon Quilters of San Diego; The Progressive Pictorial Quilt, donated by Caron Mosey; Rococo Islands, donated by Mary Jo Dalrymple; Sophistication, donated by Mr. & Mrs. Mark Wiseman; Square within a Square within a Square, donated by Ruth Britton Smalley; Stella Antigua, donated by Hanne Vibeke de Koning-Stapel; Tradition in the Attic, donated by Trigg County Quilters; Traditional Bouquet, donated by Ludmila Uspenskaya.

DONATED BY SCHROEDER PUBLISHING

Aletsch, Air Show, Ancient Directions, Ann Orr's "Ye Olde Sampler," Autumn Radiance, Basket of Flowers, Baskets I, Beach Roses, The Blade, Blazing Splendor, Brown County Log Cabins, Buffalo Magic, Cityscape, Clamshell, Community Barn Raising, Corn Crib, Country Garden, Crossings, Diffractions III, Distant Closeness, Double Wedding Ring, Escape from Circle City, Feathered Friends, Feathered Star Sampler, Flower Basket, Flower Basket Sampler, Freedom's Cascade, Galaxy of Quilters, Grandmother's Engagement Ring (Statz), Grandmother's Engagement Ring (Sepulvado), Hearts & Stars, Incantation, Indian Crazy, Lancaster County Rose, Lilies of Autumn, A Little Bit of Candlewicking, Maltese Cross, Many Stars, Maple Leaf, Mariner's Compass, May Shadows, Morisco, Nature's Walk, Ne'er Encounter Pain, Neon Nights, New York Beauty, Night and Noon Variation, Night Bloom, Nosegay, Nothing Gold Can Stay, Ohio Bride's Quilt, Orchard Beauty, Oriental Poppy, Our Secret Garden, Outlooks, Peace and Love, Persian Paradise, Phoenix Rising, Pineapple Log Cabin, President's Wreath Variation, Prosperity, Quilted Counterpane, Reach for the Stars, Red Poppies, Ribbons and Roses, Rising Moons, Rosemaling Inspiration, Roses by Starlight, Roses for a June Bride, Saturn's Rings, Serenity II: Life in My Pond, Shadow Baltimore Bride, Splendor of the Rajahs, Springtime Sampler, Stained Glass Windows, Star Bright, Star-Crossed, Starburst, Starry, Starry Night, Strawberry Sundae, Submergence, Sunset Kites, Taos Tapestry, Terrarium, Three for the Crown, Tranquility, Trip around the World, Tulips in a Basket, Twelve Days of Christmas, Up, Up, and Away, Voice of Freedom, When Grandmother's Lily Garden Blooms, Zinnias in the Windows of My Log Cabin.

DONATED BY BILL & MEREDITH SCHROEDER

Amish Mutual Aid, Colonial Lady, Complimentary Composition, Crown of Cerise, Desert Dusk, Discovery, Dreamcatcher, Escapade, Fear of the Dark, Grace, Here Between, Indian Summer, Pandas 'Round the World, Reflection #3.

PURCHASED BY MAQS WITH FUNDS DONATED FOR THE PURCHASES BY BILL SCHROEDER:

Baskets and the Corn, Boat in a Bottle Sampler, Celebration, Chips and Whetstones, Country School, Feathered Star Bouquet, Garden Party, Ice Fantasia, The Map Makers, Night Beacons III, Restoring the Balance, Silversword – Degener's Dream, Waste Not, Want Not.

DONATED THROUGH AQS QUILT SHOW PURCHASE AWARDS:

Air Show; Ancient Directions; Autumn Radiance; Baltimore Remembered; The Beatles Quilt; Bed of Peonies; The Beginnings; Birds of a Different Color; Blue Earth Filled with Water and Flowers; Blueberry Morning, Butternut Summer; Cabins in the Cosmos; Conway Album (I'm Not from Baltimore); Corona II: Solar Eclipse; Dawn Splendor; Descending Visions; Dot's Vintage 1983; Enlightenment; Floral Urns; Garden Maze; Goato and Friends; Gypsy in My Soul; Hammered at Home; Heliacal Rise; Hot Fun; It's Not Summer Yet; Jelly Bean; Joie de Vie – Joy of Life; Kettle Moraine Star; Le Jardin de Nos Reves; Lilies Are Forever; Lime Light, Looking Back on Broken Promises; Midwinter Night's Dream; Migration #2; Momma's Garden; Mother's Day; Mount Pleasant Miners; October Morning; One Fish, Two Fish, Red Fish, Blue Fish; Oriental Fantasy; Pop Stars; Raggedy Sun Worshippers; The Space Quilt, Spice of Life, Spring Flower Baskets; Spring Winds; Star Flower, Sun-Bathing Blue Tit, Sunburst Quilt; Sweetheart on Parade; Tennessee Pink Marble; Totem, Toujours Nouveau; Tulips Aglow; Victorian Fantasy of Feathers and Lace; Vintage Rose Garden; Wild Rose; Who's Your Poppy?.

QUILTS PURCHASED BY MAQS IN "10 QUILTS FOR 10 YEARS CAMPAIGN"

A Li'l Bit Crazy Two; Listen to Your Mother, sponsored by Mollie & Bill Heron and John & Helen Thompson; The Mountain and the Magic: Night Lights; Move Over Matisse I; Na Pali sponsored by Mollie & Bill Heron and John & Helen Thompson; New Directions, sponsored by Bill Schroeder; On Wednesday Morning; Precipice, sponsored in part by Dr. Gerald & Arlene Blackburn; Star of Chamblie, sponsored by Bill Schroeder; Trees: Summer/Winter, sponsored by Bill Schroeder.

QUILTS PURCHASED BY MAQS

Snow Scapes by Jo Diggs.

MAQS Staff

S taff, whether paid or volunteer, have played a key role in the Museum of the American Quilter's Society's celebration of quilts, quiltmakers, and quiltmaking.

MAQS opened its doors in 1991, governed by a four-member board, with the following paid staff: a gift shop sales person, a front desk receptionist, an assistant director, a part-time visitor services assistant, a building maintenance person; assisted by these unpaid staff: a part-time executive director on loan from AQS and many community volunteers.

The museum has since developed its board to include eight members, its paid staff to include 18 full and part-time members, and its year-round volunteer corps to include over 150.

A group of volunteers who have undergone in-depth training now provide guided tours for the thousands of children and adults to visit the museum in groups. National quilt leaders also volunteer their time, assisting with planning and special projects, such as the Shannon-Ross and Patricia J. Morris Scholarship Fund programs, for which Julie Powell, Katy Christopherson, and Caryl Bryer Fallert review applications.

The board of directors provides valuable expertise, experience, ideas, and contacts. They are responsible for the museum's continuing commitment to contemporary quilting and excellence in collection care and programs.

In addition, MAQS relies on regional and national advisory groups for additional advice and direction. In 1997, over 40 stakeholders from around the country spent two days at MAQS envisioning the institution's future, and out of that planning have grown a wide array of new projects and initiatives. In 2004, the board of directors and a planning consultant reviewed progress toward the goals conceived in 1997 and set new priorities for the next five years.

The following pages look at the range of MAQS programming during these first 10 years and some of the people connected with it.

MAQS STAFF, December 2000. Front Row (l to r): Sherry Johnston, Kitty Shadle, Melanie Ramage, Lisa Vandiver, Millie Ford, Dorisanna Conner, Carolyn Leidecker, Ruby Armstrong, Rosemary Harris. Back Row (l to r): Susan Dorris, Payne Sage, Victoria Faoro, Johannah Huyck, Alice Tabor. Not Pictured: Loretta Alveary, Jewel Reid, Paul Weaver, Dennis Harrison.
PHOTO: STACY ROGERS

MAQS STAFF, December 2004. Jessica Byassee, Carolyn Carver, Carrie Cox, Rosemary Harris, Donna-Maria Walker, Pamela Hill, Johannah Huyck, Sherry Johnson, Steve Miller, Linda Pollender, Melanie Ramage, Jewel Reid, Garth Spees, Martha Stewart, Alice Tabor, Judy Schwender, and Susan Talbot-Stanaway, Executive Director.

MIDDLE: **Meredith Schroeder, president of the board of directors, addresses volunteers during the December 2000 volunteer recognition reception held in the museum's lobby, amid a display of holiday quilts made by MAQS volunteers.**
PHOTO: STACY ROGERS

BOTTOM: **MAQS volunteers mingling with quilt lenders and community members during a lobby reception held in 1999 in conjunction with Between the Rivers, a MAQS exhibit that explored quiltmaking in the communities of Western Kentucky that were relocated when Land Between the Lakes was established following the creation of Kentucky and Barkley Lakes.**

TOP: **The Color Orange exhibit, one of the opening exhibits at MAQS in April 1991. The black lines on the carpet are tape lines that were placed to limit how close visitors could stand to view quilts on display.**

CENTER: **Garment and quilt on display in From Russia to Kentucky with Style: Quilts & Garments by Russian Designers (1992). This first display of wearable art at MAQS was followed by Wonderful Wearables, an exhibit curated by Virginia Avery.**

BOTTOM: **Quilt collectors Paul D. Pilgrim (left) and Gerald E. Roy standing behind the signature piece in The Log Cabin Returns to Kentucky (1992).**

MAQS *Exhibits*

1991

Quilts by 1991 AQS Quilt Show Instructors, 04/25/91 – 06/01/91

The Color Orange, curated by Paul D. Pilgrim & Gerald E. Roy, 04/25/91 – 07/06/91

Mary Schafer Quilts, curated by Joe Cunningham & Gwen Marston, 04/25/91 – 08/03/91

Quilts by AQS Authors, 04/25/91 – 06/01/91

Southern Quilts: A New View, organized by the Hunter Museum of Art, Chattanooga, TN, 07/09/91 – 08/24/91

Heartland Quilters: An Exhibit by Regional Guilds, coordinated by Sharee Dawn Roberts, 08/27/91 – 09/14/91

Nineteenth-Century Quilts from Local Collections, curated by MAQS, 08/10/91 – 12/11/91

In Response to Their World, curated by MAQS, 09/21/91 – 12/28/91

Fifteen Years Later: Bicentennial Quilts, curated by MAQS, 12/07/91 – 04/11/92

A Collector's Choice: Antique Quilts from the Herbert Wallerstein Collection, 12/14/91 – 4/04/92

1992

Material Connections: Contemporary Quilts by the North Texas Quilt Artists, coordinated by Barbara Oliver Hartman, 06/13/92 – 08/29/92

From Russia to Kentucky with Style: Quilts & Garments by Russian Designers, coordinated by Ludmila Bokov, 01/04/92 – 02/15/92

From Hearts & Hands: Japanese Quilts, curated by Atsuko Hashiura, 02/22/92 – 06/06/92

Wonderful Wearables, curated by Virginia Avery, 02/22/92 – 06/06/92

The Log Cabin Returns to Kentucky: Quilts from the Pilgrim/Roy Collection, curated by Paul D. Pilgrim & Gerald E. Roy, 04/16/92 – 08/08/92

Quilts from the Mina Newman White Collection, 08/15/92 – 01/02/93

More Than Just Something to Keep You Warm: Traditions and Change in African–American Quilting, curated by Roland Freeman, 09/26/92 – 01/23/93

1993

Heartland Quilts '93, coordinated by MAQS, 01/30/93 – 04/10/93

Firestorm, curated by Mary Mashuta, 01/30/93 – 04/10/93

Old and New: A Similar View (pairing of quilts from the MAQS Collection with antique Pilgrim/Roy Collection quilts), curated by Paul D. Pilgrim & Gerald E. Roy, 03/13/93 – 06/17/93

Visions: The Art of the Quilt, coordinated by Quilt San Diego, 04/17/93 – 08/28/93

A Matter of Scale: Historical Miniatures, by Tina Gravatt (miniature quilts on appropriate small-scale beds, with full-size quilts of the same design), 06/26/93 – 10/02/93

Nancy Crow: Work in Transition, curated by Nancy Crow, 09/04/93 – 01/01/94

Old & New: A Similar View, curated by Paul D. Pilgrim and Gerald E. Roy, 10/16/93 – 01/15/94

1994

Over, Under, Around & Through: Quilts from the Fabric Vision Group (MO) and the Colorado Connection (CO), coordinated by Lois T. Smith & Patty Hawkins, 01/08/94 – 04/02/94

New Jersey Quilts: 1800 – 1935, curated by the New Jersey Quilt Project, 01/22/94 – 04/09/94

A Celebration of Excellence, AQS purchase award winners, each displayed with a new quilt by the maker, curated by MAQS, 03/26/94 – 06/18/94

Quilt National '94, coordinated by Dairy Barn Southeastern Ohio Cultural Arts Center, 04/09/94 – 05/20/94

Double Wedding Ring Quilts: New Quilts from an Old Favorite, MAQS contest exhibit, 04/27/94 – 08/20/94

Baltimore Album Revival, curated by Elly Sienkiewicz, 05/20/94 – 09/16/94

School Block Challenge '94, MAQS contest exhibit, 06/27/94 – 11/04/94

Victorian Quilts – 1775 – 1900: They Aren't All Crazy, curated by Paul D. Pilgrim & Gerald E. Roy, 08/27/94 – 01/14/95

Hurricane Andrew Quilts, quilts by South East Art Quilters, 09/17/94 – 01/02/95

1995

Sue Benner – Quilts: A Vibrant Journal, organized by the Neville Public Museum, WI, 09/17/94 – 01/07/95

Heartland Quilts '95, coordinated by MAQS, 01/14/95 – 03/11/95

Log Cabin Quilts: New Quilts from an Old Favorite, MAQS contest exhibit, 03/04/95 – 06/03/95

Contemporary Quilts from the James Collection, curated by Penny McMorris, 03/18/95 – 06/17/95

Gatherings: America's Quilt Heritage, curated by Paul D. Pilgrim & Gerald E. Roy, 4/15/95 – 08/12/95

Quilts by Members of Studio Art Quilt Associates, 06/24/95 – 10/27/95

Dreams & Fantasies: Quilts by Ludmila Uspenskaya, curated by Marilyn Henrion, 06/10/95 – 08/19/95

Common Threads: Quilts and Textiles from the Miriam Tuska Collection, curated by Helen Thompson, 08/28/95 – 12/30/95

TOP: **Philadelphia, PA, quiltmaker and collector Tina Gravatt with a sample of the miniature quilts and doll beds displayed at MAQS in A Matter of Scale: Historical Miniatures (1993).**

CENTER: **Entries in the School Block Challenge '94 contest sponsored by P&B Textiles, on display in the museum's lobby (1994). This annual contest and exhibit initiated in 1994 has grown to include entries from schools in a five-state region, with continued sponsorship by P&B Textiles.**

BOTTOM: **Nancy Crow lectured and taught a workshop at MAQS while her exhibit, Nancy Crow: Work in Transition (1994), was on display. AQS published a catalog featuring Crow's work.**

TOP: **Common Threads: Quilts & Textiles from the Miriam Tuska Collection** (1995) featured a wide range of textiles that had captured the interest of this collector, including quilts, stitched garments, and paisley shawls.

CENTER: For this retrospective exhibit, **Michael James: Studio Quilts – 25 Years** (1999), curatorial staff were convinced to paint the galleries a light blue, and use lettering applied directly to the exhibit wall, changing the way future MAQS exhibits would be installed.

BOTTOM: **The Herrick Log Cabin**, a quilt central to the Pilgrim/Roy Collection, is featured again at MAQS in this latest exhibit from this collection entitled **Classic Quilts from the Pilgrim/Roy Collection** (2000 & 2001).

Anna Williams: Quilts & Influences, coordinated by Katherine Watts, 09/16/95 – 01/01/96

Flowers & Quilts: A Salute to Martha Stewart, curated by MAQS, 10/05/95 – 10/07/95

1996

Ohio Star Quilts: New Quilts from an Old Favorite, MAQS contest exhibit, 01/06/96 – 05/11/96

Broadway Haiku, coordinated by the Manhattan Quilters Guild, 01/06/96 – 05/11/96

Quilts from the Mountain Mist Historical Collection, 01/20/96 – 03/02/96

Heartland Quilts '96, coordinated by MAQS, 01/13/96 – 03/02/96

Caryl Bryer Fallert: A Spectrum of Quilts, 1983 – 1995, 03/09/96 – 06/15/96

Scouts & Quilts: A Scout Is Helpful, curated by the National Boy Scout Museum, 03/23/96 – 05/25/96

Amish Kinder Komforts: Quilts from the Sara Miller Collection, curated by Bettina Havig, 05/18/96 – 08/31/96

Pilgrim's Progress: Quilts by Paul D. Pilgrim, curated by Gerald E. Roy, 06/22/96 – 09/14/96

The Architecture of Quilts, coordinated by the Gibbs Museum of Art, SC, 06/22/96 – 09/14/96

Campaign Voices – Ballot Choices: Political Keepsakes & Quilts, curated by Julie and Robin Powell, 09/07/96 – 01/04/97

1997

The Quilts of Ruth B. McDowell, curated by MAQS, 09/26/96 – 01/18/97

School Block Challenge '97, MAQS contest exhibit, 01/11/97 – 03/15/97

Antique Mariner's Compass Quilts, curated by MAQS, 01/25/97 – 05/24/97

Mariner's Compass Quilts: New Quilts from an Old Favorite, MAQS contest exhibit, 01/25/97 – 05/24/97

Rural Legacy: Quilts by Rella Thompson & Geneva Alston, Franklin County, NC, curated by Kathlyn Sullivan, 01/11/97 – 03/15/97

Quilters Make Their Mark: Twentieth Century Quilts, 1900 – 1970, curated by Joyce Gross & Cuesta Benberry, 03/22/97 – 06/28/97

On the Edge: Northwest Quilt Art, quilts by Contemporary Quilt Art Association, WA, 05/31/97 – 07/18/97

Grand & Glorious: Four Block Quilts from the Collection of Linda Carlson, 07/05/97 – 09/13/97

Celebrating MAQS/Schroeder Collection (all quilts in the collection), 09/20/97 – 01/17/98

1998

Storybook Quilts by Marion Cheever Whitesides, curated by Naida T. Patterson, 01/24/98 – 03/28/98

Bible Blocks, collection of Dorothy Bond, 01/24/98 – 03/28/98

School Block Challenge '98, MAQS contest exhibit, 02/07/98 – 03/21/98

Masterpiece Quilts & Their Makers, coordinated by the National Quilting Association, 03/28/98 – 06/27/98

Pineapple Quilts: New Quilts from an Old Favorite, MAQS contest exhibit, 04/04/98 – 07/18/98

Antique Pineapple Quilts, curated by MAQS, 04/04/98 – 07/18/98

Antique Quilts from the Shelly Zegart Collection, 04/04/98 – 07/18/98

Together and Apart: Studio Art Quilts from New Image, 07/25/98 – 11/07/98

Variations on a Theme: Miniature Quilts by Tina Gravatt, 08/08/98 – 01/09/99

5 x 5: Five Maine Quilters Respond to Ecclesiastes 3:1-11, coordinated by Diane Hire, 11/14/98 – 02/20/99

Patchworks of Remembrance & Hope, coordinated by MAQS, 11/14/98 – 02/20/99

1999

School Block Challenge '99, MAQS contest exhibit, 01/16/99 – 03/13/99

Quilts from the Morrilton School Quilt Collection, coordinated by Jim Gatlin, 01/16/99 – 03/13/99

Michael James: Studio Quilts – 25 Years, 02/27/99 – 05/22/99

Kaleidoscopes Quilts: New Quilts from an Old Favorite, MAQS contest exhibit, 03/20/99 –06/26/99

Quilts & Kaleidoscopes, curated by Paula Nadelstern, featuring her kaleidoscope quilts and actual kaleidoscopes, 03/20/99 – 06/26/99

Glorious Chintz: Early 19th Century Quilts from the Byron & Sara Dillow Collection, 08/01/99 – 10/23/99

Deidre Scherer – Layered Visions: Works in Fabric and Thread, 05/29/99 – 09/04/99

Back to School. . . Tactile Academics, invitational exhibit curated by Patricia J. Morris & Jeannette Muir, 09/11/99 – 01/08/00

Between the Rivers: Quilts & Communities, 1800's – 1960's, curated by MAQS, 10/30/99 – 01/29/00

2000

Storm at Sea Quilts: New Quilts from an Old Favorite, MAQS contest exhibit, 01/15/00 – 05/13/00

Old & New, East & West: Japanese Quilts by the Three Y's, quilts by Yumiko Hirasawa, Yoko Kyono & Yukiko Hirano, 01/15/00 – 02/26/00

Fabric Storyscapes by Franklin Elementary School Students, Madison, Wisconsin, coordinated by Nancy Daly & Cinda W. Dalebroux, 02/05/00 – 03/11/00

School Block Challenge 2000, MAQS contest exhibit, 02/05/00 – 03/11/00

Quilts by Doreen Speckmann, curated by Gerald E. Roy, 03/04/00 – 09/16/00

Quilts Uncovered: AQSG Celebrates 20 Years of Quilt Scholarship, curated by Nancy Hornback & Jennifer Goldsbrough, 03/18/00 – 07/08/00

A Tribute to Doreen Speckmann, curated by Gerald E. Roy, 05/20/00 – 09/16/00

Classic Quilts from the Pilgrim-Roy Collection, curated by Gerald E. Roy, 07/15/00 – 10/28/00

The Last Year: Surrounded by Family & Friends, works by Deidre Scherer, 09/23/00 – 10/21/00

Narrative Portraits, quilts by FACET, 09/23/00 – 02/03/01

Windy City Blues, quilts by FACET, 10/28/00 – 02/03/01

Blending the Old & the New: Quilts by Paul D. Pilgrim, curated by Gerald. E Roy, 11/04/00 – 01/06/01

2001

Quilted Illustrations by Adrienne Yorinks, curated by MAQS, 01/13/01–03/17/01

Quilts across America, traveled by American Folk Art Museum, 01/13/01 – 03/04/01

School Block Challenge 2001, MAQS contest exhibit, 01/13/01 – 03/17/01

Classic Quilts from the Pilgrim-Roy Collection, curated by Gerald E. Roy, 03/17/01 – 08/11/01

Bear's Paw Quilts: New Quilts from an Old Favorite, MAQS contest exhibit, 02/10/01– 06/30/01

An Apple for the Teacher, Celebrating the Work of Patricia J. Morris, 04/00/01– 06/30/01

TOP: **Quilters Make Their Mark: Twentieth Century Quilts, 1900 – 1970, a 1997 MAQS exhibit curated by Cuesta Benberry (St. Louis, MO) and Joyce Gross (Petaluma, CA). These noted quilt historians, who have both been inducted into the Quilter's Hall of Fame, explored the roots of** today's exciting quiltmaking activity through this exhibit and a conference held in June 1997.

BOTTOM: **Deidre Scherer – Layered Visions: Works in Fabric and Thread (1999)** was a retrospective exhibit of the portraits, landscapes, and still lifes created by this Vermont artist using commercial fabrics and machine stitching. A number of the works explored subjects often avoided in today's world, such as aging and the process of dying.

TOP: **Period room setting in the 1994 MAQS exhibit Victorian Quilts, 1875 – 1900: They Aren't All Crazy, curated by Paul D. Pilgrim and Gerald E. Roy.** PHOTO: STEVE MARTIN, HENDERSON, KY.

MIDDLE: **The 1996 MAQS exhibit Ballot Choices, Campaign Choices: Political Keepsakes & Quilts, curated by Julie and Robin Powell, featured a wonderful combination of such objects as this Henry Clay quilt and array of political keepsakes.**

BOTTOM: **Kaleidoscope Quilts: New Quilts from an Old Favorite** contest exhibit in 1999, featured a hands-on exhibit of contemporary kaleidoscopes curated by Paula Nadelstern.

Companions & Choices: Quilts & Paintings, coordinated by Rod Bufffington, 07/07/01 – 10/22/01

Oxymorons: Absurdly Logical Quilts, curated by The Renegades, 08/18/01 – 01/12/02

Quilts Expressively Korean, 10/27/01 – 03/09/02

2002

Tumbling Blocks: New Quilts from an Old Favorite, 03//02/02 – 06/20/02

Professional Art Quilt Alliance: Small Works, curated by the Professional Art Quilt Alliance, 03/02/02 – 06/20/02

Plain & Fancy: Vermont State Quiltsearch Project, 03/16/02 – 10/19/02

Piece Be Still, 06/29/02 – 01/04/03

Marriage of Heaven and Earth, 09/21/02 – 01/04/03

Two Visionaries: Frances Brand and Molly Upton, 10/26/02 – 03/08/03

2003

Breaking from Tradition: Quilt Explorations by Terri Hancock Mangat, Arturo Sandoval, and Zelda Tannebaum, 01/11/03 – 02/22/03

School Block Challenge, 01/11/03 – 02/22/03

Feathered Star: New Quilts from an Old Favorite, 03/01/02 – 06/21/03

In Fine Feather: Antique Feathered Star Quilts, curated by Marsha McCloskey, 03/01/03 – 06/21/03

Man Made, 03/15/03 – 07/12/03

Kentucky: A Cornerstone for Expansion, 04/15/03 – 08/18/03

The Garden View, 06/28/03 – 09/27/03

Quilted Memories of Kentucky, curated by Helen Thompson, 07/19/03 – 11/29/03

Lewis & Clark Expedition Quilts, 10/04/03 – 01/04/04

Red & White, curated by Ann Hazelwood, 12/06/03 – 03/06/04

2004

School Block Challenge, 01/10/04 – 02/21/04

Monkey Wrench: New Quilts from an Old Favorite, 02/28/04 – 06/05/04

Power for Change: Quilting and the Sewing Machine, 03/13/04 – 07/03/04

Prize-Winning Quilters & Their Quilts: 20th Anniversary Exhibition, 03/27/04 – 07/31/04

In a Thousand Pieces: Quilts from Laura Fisher Antique Quilts and Americana, 04/10/04 – 06/05/04

The Fabric of Jazz: A Tribute to the Genius of American Music, 06/12/04 – 09/25/04

Making Do and Making Beautiful: 100 Years of Quilts, 07/15/04 – 09/05/04

Amish Quilts from the Permanent Collection, 07/15/04 – 09/05/04

Handkerchief Quilts by Pat Gardner, 09/10/04 – 11/24/04

Gifts of Love: Quilts by Kathy McNeil, 10/01/04 – 01/08/05

Doll Quilts from the Collection of Mary Ghormley, 12/04/04 – 02/23/05

THEMES AND SPONSORS FOR THE NEW QUILTS FROM AN OLD FAVORITE CONTEST

CURRENT YEAR
2004 – Monkey Wrench
Fairfield Processing Corp.,
Janome, Timeless Treasures

1994 – Double Wedding Ring
Fabric Traditions, Fairfield Processing Corp.,
New Home Janome

1995 – Log Cabin
Fabric Traditions, Fairfield Processing Corp.,
New Home Janome

1996 – Ohio Star
Fabric Traditions, Fairfield Processing Corp.,
New Home Janome

1997 – Mariner's Compass
Fabric Traditions, Fairfield Processing Corp.,
New Home Janome

1998 – Pineapple
Fabric Traditions, Fairfield Processing Corp.,
New Home Janome

1999 – Kaleidoscope
Fabric Traditions/Classic Traditions,
Fairfield Processing Corp., New Home Janome

2000 – Storm at Sea
Fairfield Processing Corp., Janome,
Marcus Brothers Textiles

2001 – Bear's Paw
Fairfield Processing Corp.,
Janome, Marcus Brothers Textiles

2002 – Tumbling Block
Fairfield Processing Corp.,
Janome, Marcus Brothers Textiles

2003 – Feathered Star
Fairfield Processing Corp.,
Janome, Marcus Brothers Textiles

MAQS stimulates quiltmaking activity through several annual contests made possible by corporate sponsorship.

SCHOOL BLOCK CHALLENGE CONTEST

Each year MAQS challenges students in pre-K through grade 12 who attend schools within a 300-mile radius of Paducah to create 16" quilt blocks using three challenge fabrics supplied by the contest's sponsor, P&B TEXTILES. Students are required to work in groups of at least two, and each class can submit up to three blocks for competition and display at MAQS. Blocks are entered in three age categories and award winners are selected in each category. All blocks submitted to MAQS are displayed for the exhibit and the winning blocks are displayed for the remainder of the year.

NEW QUILTS FROM AN OLD FAVORITE

An annual contest for adult quiltmakers challenges them to use a particular traditional block pattern to develop an innovative quilt. A different block is designated as the theme block of each year. This contest and the resulting traveling exhibit provide a wonderful look at the way quiltmakers build on the tradition, making the design their own as they use it in their quilt.

Award Winners

FIRST PLACE
1994 – Keiko Goke, Sendai, Miyagi, Japan
1995 – Keiko Goke, Sendai, Miyagi, Japan
1996 – Izumi Takamori, Tokyo, Japan
1997 – Debbie Hern, Dousman, WI
1998 – Mary Ann Herndon, Houston, TX
1999 – Barbara Oliver Hartman, Flower Mound, TX
2000 – Gwenfai Rees Griffiths, Abergele, Wales
2001 – Claudia Clark Myers, Duluth, MN
2002 – Barbara Oliver Hartman, Flower Mound, TX
2003 – Sherri Bain Driver, Englewood, CO
2004 – Gwenfai Rees Griffiths, Abergele, Wales

SECOND PLACE
1994 – Nancy Lambert, Mequon, WI
1995 – Laura Murray, Minneapolis, MN
1996 – Maggie Potter, Walnut Creek, CA
1997 – Gene P. H. Ives, Alexandria, VA
1998 – Dixie Haywood, Pensacola, FL
1999 – Izumi Takamori, Tokyo, Japan
2000 – Sue Turnquist, Harrisburg, MO
2001 – Gayle Wallace & Gertrude Embree, Shreveport, LA
2002 – D. Nadine Ruggles, Gerlingen, Germany
2003 – Barbara Oliver Hartman, Flower Mound, TX
2004 – Sherri Bain Driver, Centennial, CO

THIRD PLACE
1994 – Susan Stein, St. Paul, MN
1995 – Barbara T. Kaempfer, Mettmenstetten, Switzerland
1996 – Sue Spigel, Christchurch, New Zealand
1997 – Ans Schipper-Vermeiren, Hagestein, The Netherlands
1998 – Judy Sogn, Seattle, WA
1999 – Sachiko Suzuki, Chiba, Japan
2000 – Inge Mardal & Steen Hougs, Brussels, Belgium
2001 – Vicky Lawrence, Overbrook, KS
2002 – Cindy Vough, Nicholasville, KY
2003 – Nancy Lambert, Pittsburgh, PA
2004 – Patricia Dowling, Callahan, FL

From the start, MAQS has been dedicated to education, and workshops and conferences have played an important role in programming.

In 1992 a series of workshops for learning design and quilt construction techniques was begun, with three to five-day opportunities to study with leading quiltmakers. Generally 20 to 25 students are involved with each workshop, during which they totally immerse themselves in quiltmaking, arriving before 8 a.m. and often reluctantly leaving the museum's classrooms at 9 p.m.

Shannon-Ross Fund scholarships are available on a competitive basis to enable a wider range of students to participate. The Shannon-Ross Scholarship Program was established in 1993 through a generous initial donation from Jonathan Shannon and Jeffrey Ross of Phoenix, Arizona. Jonathan donated his $15,000 Best of Show award from the 1993 AQS Quilt Show & Contest. This money was matched by MAQS co-founders Bill and Meredith Schroeder, and contributed to by other individuals. As interest is earned, it is used to fund as many $400 scholarships as possible for quiltmaking students participating in in-depth workshops at MAQS.

MAQS also holds focused conferences, often related to special exhibits. Perhaps the largest conference was the one held in conjunction with Gatherings: America's Quilt Heritage, an exhibit developed by MAQS with support from the Lila Wallace Reader's Digest Fund, that traveled across the country to other museums. This conference held in 1995 brought together the project's advisory team and representatives from many of our country's state quilt documentation projects.

MAQS also provides educational experiences for young people, through Quilt Camps for Kids workshops taught by AQS show chair Bonnie Browning each July.

ABOVE: **During a 1994 workshop, a group of students gather around Elly Sienkiewicz as she demonstrates a hand-appliqué technique. The limited class size and multi-day format of MAQS quiltmaking workshops enable students to explore topics or techniques in depth.**

MAQS Conferences and *Workshops*

1992
Michael James (MA), Visual Dynamics: Studies in Line, Space, Texture and Pattern, 4-day workshop
Joen Wolfrom (WA), Landscapes & Illusions, 4-day workshop
Caryl Bryer Fallert (IL), String Piecing and Beyond: Personal Expression with Innovative Techniques, 4-day workshop
Debra Wagner (MN), Whigs Defeat or Engagement Ring, 4-day workshop
David Walker (OH), Narrative Abstractions: Expressing Personal Images, 4-day workshop
Nancy Crow (OH), Transitional Class: How to Make Traditional Blocks Look Contemporary, 4-day workshop
Terrie H. Mangat (OH), Mixed Media Quiltmaking, 4-day workshop
Nancy Pearson (IL), Let's Sew a Garden, 4-day workshop

1993
African American Quilters Forum: Tradition and Change in African-American Quilting, 2-day conference
Judi Warren [Blaydon] (OH), Quilt Design, 3-day workshop
Nancy Halpern (MA), Architectural Forms for Quilts, 3-day workshop
Carolyn Dahl (TX) Dye Painting with and without Resists, 4-day workshop
Nancy Crow (OH), Improvisations! Let's Experiment, 5-day workshop
Rosalie Dace & Odette Tolksdorf (South Africa), Africa Goes Crazy, 2-day workshop & 2-day workshop

1994
Elly Sienkiewicz (Washington, DC), Dimensional Appliqué: Baskets, Blooms & Baltimore Borders, 4-day workshop
Caryl Bryer Fallert (IL), Beyond the Grid: Personal Expression with Innovative Techniques, 4-day workshop
Nancy Pearson (IL), Beauty of the Seasons Quilt, 4-day workshop
Yvonne Porcella (CA), Innovative Pieced Clothing, 4-day workshop

1995
Klaudeen Hansen (WI), Make a Mystery Quilt, 1-day workshop
Patricia Morris (NJ), Perfect Your Quilting Stitch, 1-day workshop
Gatherings Celebration Weekend, 3-day conference sponsored by Benartex, Inc.
Annual AQSG Seminar, hosted by MAQS, 3-day conference

1996
Nancy Pearson (IL), Floral Appliqué, 3-day workshop
Bettina Havig (MO), Amish Quilts and Quilt Motifs, 1-day workshop & Waste Not Want Not, 1-day workshop
Caryl Bryer Fallert (IL), Creative String Piecing, 4-day workshop
Shari Cole (New Zealand), Diagonal Plaited Colorwash, 1-day workshop & Plaited Colorwash Patchwork, 2-day workshop
Ruth McDowell (MA), Designing with Symmetry, 3-day workshop
Elly Sienkiewicz (Wash. DC), A Textured Appliqué Album Block, 3-day workshop

1997
Michael James (MA), Color Dynamics & Expression Integrating Color, Pattern, and Vision, 3-day workshop
Judy Mathieson, Mariner's Compass and Beyond, 3-day workshop
Margaret Miller, Quilts from the Cutting Wedge, 3-day workshop
Katie Pasquini Masopust (NM), Fractured Landscapes, 3-day workshop
Envisioning Our Future, 2-day museum planning conference with QM2 consultants
Quilters Make Their Mark: Twentieth Century Quilts, 1900 – 1970, 2-day conference coordinated by Joyce Gross and Cuesta Benberry

1998

Michael James (MA), Color Dynamics and Expression, 3-day workshop
Elly Sienkiewicz (Wash. DC), Innovative Heirloom Appliqué, 3-day workshop
Nancy Pearson (IL), Floral Appliqué, 3-day workshop
Caryl Bryer Fallert (IL), Creative Free-Form Piecing, 4-day workshop
Caryl Bryer Fallert (IL), Creative Free-Form Piecing, 4-day workshop (second session)
Katie Pasquini Masopust (NM), Fractured Landscapes, 3-day workshop
Ruth B. McDowell (MA), Designing from Nature, 4-day workshop

1999

Caryl Bryer Fallert (IL), Creative Free-Form Piecing, 4-day workshop
Libby Lehman (TX), Threadplay: Go For It!, 3-day workshop
Michael James (MA), Fabric Interplay, 3-day workshop
Nancy Crow (OH), Improvisations, 5-day workshop
Ruth B. McDowell (MA), Designing from Nature, 4-day workshop

2000

Ruth B. McDowell (MA), Designing from Nature, 4-day workshop
Libby Lehman (TX), Threadplay, 3-day workshop
Jo Diggs (ME), Layered Appliqué, 3-day workshop
Caryl Bryer Fallert (IL), Creative Free-Form Piecing, 4-day workshop
Nancy Pearson (IL), Floral Appliqué, 3-day workshop
Elizabeth Busch (ME), Painted Quilts: Mixing It All Up, 4-day workshop
Elly Sienkiewicz (Wash. DC), Baltimore Appliqué, 3-day workshop

2001

Paula Nadelstern (NY), Kaleidoscope Quilts, 3-day workshop
Caryl Bryer Fallert (IL), Creative Free-Form Piecing, 4-day workshop
Elizabeth Busch (ME), Painted Quilts: Mixing It All Up, 4-day workshop
Jo Diggs (ME), Layered Landscape Appliqué, 3-day workshop
Ruth B. McDowell (MA), Designing from Nature, 4-day workshop
David Walker (OH), Expressive Machine Appliqué Techniques, 3-day workshop

2002

Libby Lehman (TX), Threadplay, 3-day workshop
Nancy Pearson (IL), Floral Appliqué, 3-day workshop
Ruth B. McDowell (MA), Designing from Nature, 5-day workshop
Michael James (NE), Visual Dynamics: Studies in Line, Space, Texture, and Pattern, 4-day workshop
Nancy Crow (OH), Exploration of Strip-Piecing in Contemporary Quiltmaking, 5-day workshop
Elly Sienkiewicz, (Wash. DC), Urn of Fruit Still Life by Theorem Appliqué, 3-day workshop

2003

Caryl Bryer Fallert (IL), Creative Free-form Piecing and Design, 5-day workshop
Diane Gaudynski (WI), Machine Quilting: A New Tradition, 3-day workshop
Irma Gail Hatcher (AR), Basket with 3-D Blooms, Dogtooth Border, Trapunto, and More, 3-day workshop
Ruth McDowell (MA), Designing from Nature, 5-day workshop
Sue Nickels (MI), Machine Appliqué–Techniques used in THE BEATLES QUILT, 3-day workshop

2004

Caryl Bryer Fallert (IL), Creative Free-form Piecing and Design, 5-day workshop
Diane Gaudynski (WI), Machine Quilting: A New Tradition, 3-day workshop
Ruth McDowell (MA), Designing from Nature, 5-day workshop
Kathy McNeil (ST), Pictorial Quilts from Front to Back, 3-day workshop
Nancy Pearson (IL), Floral Appliqué, 3-day workshop
Velda Newman (CA), Layers: Color, Shape, Texture & Collage, 3-day workshop

Corporate sponsorship makes it possible for MAQS to hold quality in-depth workshops that are affordable for quilters.

Sponsorship of the series began in 1996 – 97. Sponsors have been:

1996 – 97
Springs Fabrics, Olfa Products Group, Pfaff American Sales

1997 – 98
Springs Fabrics, Olfa Products Group, Pfaff American Sales

1998 – 99
Olfa Products Group, Pfaff American Sales, Quilters Only

1999 – 00
Olfa Products Group, Pfaff American Sales, Clotilde/ Quilts & Other Comforts

2000 – 01
Moda Fabrics, Olfa Products Group, Pfaff American Sales

2001 – 02
Flynn Quilt Frame Company, Olfa Products Group, Pfaff American Sales

ABOVE: **Students in one of Caryl Bryer Fallert's Creative Free-Form Piecing workshops gather for a group photo with the sponsor sign.**

TOP: **Members of the National Advisory Group for the Gatherings: America's Quilt Heritage project during the 1995 conference: (l to r) Kathlyn Sullivan, Paul D. Pilgrim, Cuesta Benberry, Katy Christopherson, Gerald E. Roy, Sandi Fox, Helen Thompson, Victoria Faoro, Meredith Schroeder. The project involved an exhibit that traveled through 1997.**

BOTTOM: **Participants in the Gatherings Celebration Weekend conference held April 21 – 23, 1995, at MAQS, sponsored by Benartex, Inc. and held in conjunction with the Gatherings: America's Quilt Heritage exhibit.**

PHOTO: RICHARD WALKER

FIRST ROW: (l to r, on floor): Anita Shackelford, Anne Copeland, Bettina Havig, Katy Christopherson, Martha Shelton, Sandi Fox, Janet Morris, Mollie Heron, Fawn Valentine, Elsie Toyer, Helen Thompson, Mary Lohrenz, Gerald E. Roy.

SECOND ROW: Joyce Gross, Kathlyn Sullivan, Elizabeth Shelly, Margaret Ehlke, Elizabeth Suiter, Gail Hand, Cuesta Benberry, Celia LoPinto, Ann Sudduth, Bets Ramsey, Joan Knight, Juanita Reed.

THIRD ROW: Eleanor Malone, Betty Jo Haines, Helen Pfeifer, Marion Wolfe, Cynthia Holly, Ann C. Hill, Dorothy Kane, Joyce Morgan, Susanne Rose, Dorothy Zopf, Joyce Aigner, Dorothy Stish, Mary McEnaney, Anne Weaver.

FOURTH ROW: Beverly Dunivent, Victoria Faoro, Julie Powell, Anita Zaleski Weinraub, Torrey Wedge, Cheryl Kennedy, Susan Fiondella, Carolyn Lynch, Mary Ann Spencer, Sue Reich, Virginia McElroy, Thelma Baker, Gwen Meatyard, Paul D. Pilgrim, Nancy Hornback, Trudy Gallo, Marie Salazar, Charlene Kreider, Kathy Webel.

SELECTED HIGHLIGHTS
1991 – 2004

April 1991
MAQS Grand Opening

July 1991
MAQS Borrows Its First Traveling Exhibit
Southern Quilts: A New View, organized by the Hunter Museum of Art, Chattanooga, TN, was loaned to MAQS by the Hunter Museum of Art. Since then MAQS has regularly displayed exhibits and quilts loaned by other institutions across the country.

January 1992
MAQS Hosts Its First International Exhibit
Working with Ludmila Bokov of New York City, MAQS borrowed quilts and garments from Russian quilt and garment-makers to mount the exhibit From Russia to Kentucky with Style: Quilts & Garments by Russian Designers. This exhibit was followed by an exhibit of Japanese quilts curated by Atsuko Hashiura of The Hearts & Hands School, Tokyo.

March 1992
First Quiltmaking Workshops Held at MAQS
Two workshops were in progress at the same time during this first educational endeavor, one taught by Michael James, and the other by Joen Wolfrom.

July 1992
MAQS Receives Its First Grant
The Lila Wallace Reader's Digest Fund awarded MAQS its first grant, a multi-year grant to support the development of Gatherings: America's Quilt Heritage, an in-house exhibit, catalog, and traveling exhibit documenting America's quilt heritage as discovered by state quilt documentation projects around the country.

August 1992
MAQS Hires Its First Full-time Director, Patricia Young

September 1992
First Annual Educators' Reception Held at MAQS

January 16-18, 1993
African American Quilters Forum Held at MAQS
MAQS coordinated and hosted this first gathering of African-American scholars and quilters, brought together to explore tradition and change in African-American quilting. Over 175 participated in this conference held in conjunction with the exhibit More Than Just Something to Keep You Warm, curated by Roland Freeman (display at MAQS Sept 1992 – January 1993).

April 1993
Time Capsule is Buried on the Museum Grounds to Be Opened in 50 years (2043).

November 1993
First New Quilts from an Old Favorite Contest and Exhibit
The Double Wedding Ring pattern was selected for this 1994 contest challenging quiltmakers to develop an innovative quilt that clearly related to this traditional pattern. Sixteen finalists were

selected in November 1993, award-winners were selected by judges, and the exhibit was displayed at MAQS April through August 1994. Following that the contest exhibit traveled to other venues. Since then the contest has been held each year, with different themes. Current sponsors are Fairfield Processing Corp., Janome America, and Marcus Brothers Textiles.

October 1994
Victoria Faoro Named Full-time Director

December 1994
First MAQS School Block Challenge Contest Held
   This annual contest sponsored by P & B Textiles challenges students to create 16" blocks.

April 1995
Gatherings Exhibit & Celebration Weekend
   This conference was held in conjunction with the exhibit Gatherings: America's Quilt Heritage, with lectures, panel discussions, and tours. Presenters were members of the Gatherings Project's national advisory committee: Sandi Fox (CA), Cuesta Benberry (MO), Paul D. Pilgrim (CA), Gerald E. Roy (CA), Kathlyn Sullivan (NC), Helen Thompson (KY), and Katy Christopherson (KY).

March 1996
Volunteer Tour Guide Program Begun
   Training began for a group of experienced docents, to prepare them for providing guided tours for groups of children and adults visiting the museum. Since that time volunteer guides have regularly provided all such tours.

April 1996
MAQS Hosts a Tribute Exhibit and Gathering for the Late Paul D. Pilgrim

November 1996
Political Exhibit at MAQS during Clinton's Campaign Visit
   Campaign Voices – Ballot Choices: Political Keepsakes & Quilts, an exhibit of quilts, other textiles, and a wide range of fascinating memorabilia curated by Julie and Robin Powell, was on display at MAQS when President Clinton visited Paducah on his campaign trail, speaking in the downtown parking lot only a block away. Included in the exhibit was the piece "Clinton Wins," created by Ed Larson following Clinton's 1992 victory.

TOP LEFT: **Quilt sharing and discussion was an important part of the African American Quilters Forum held at MAQS in 1993.**

TOP RIGHT: **The Gatherings: America's Quilt Heritage exhibit featured one to two quilts from most of the state quilt documentation projects held around the country, including this Confederate flag quilt loaned by an Arkansas museum.**

BOTTOM: **Visitors of all ages gather around artists like weaver Dana Heath of Mayfield, KY, during the museum's annual Arts in Action Festival sponsored by Paducah Bank. The festival features over 40 artists all demonstrating their art, often with hands-on opportunities.**

PHOTO: CHARLES R. LYNCH

Close Up_____

In October 1996 MAQS teamed up with corporate sponsor PADUCAH BANK to hold the first Arts in Action Festival on the museum's grounds. This celebration of arts and community offers a day of free events for families, including admission to MAQS exhibits, demonstrations of various arts, music performances, and activities for young people. With continued support from Paducah Bank, the event is held on the second Saturday in October.

TOP: **Helen Squire, who coordinated the assembling of the MAQS Paducah's Patchworks of Remembrance & Hope, helps a young man add his quilting stitches during the Quilt-a-thon held in September 1998.**

MIDDLE: **One of many catered receptions held in the MAQS lobby during AQS Quilt Show Week to welcome quiltmakers and quilt admirers from around the world.**

PHOTO: CHARLES R. LYNCH

BOTTOM: **Gallery installation (1994) of the first New Quilts from an Old Favorite contest exhibit, Double Wedding Ring Quilts.** Subsequent themes have been Log Cabin – 1995, Ohio Star – 1996, Mariner's Compass – 1997, Pineapple – 1998, Kaleidoscope – 1999, Storm at Sea – 2000, Bear's Paw – 2001, Tumbling Blocks – 2002, Feathered Star – 2003, Monkey Wrench – 2004.

January 1996
Shannon-Ross Fund Scholarships First Given for MAQS Workshops

October 1996
First Arts in Action Festival
  In 2000 the Arts in Action Festival merged with other festivals.

June 1997
"Envisioning Our Future" Conference Held
  MAQS worked with QM2 museum management professionals bringing together about 50 local, state, and national stakeholders, to envision the best future for the museum. Following this two day retreat, goals and strategies were developed to guide activity over the upcoming years.

June 1997
"Quilters Make Their Mark: Quilting in the Twentieth Century" Conference
  Held in conjunction with an exhibit of the same title created by Joyce Gross and Cuesta Benberry, a conference was held to bring together quilt scholars and others interested in learning more about quiltmaking.

December 1997
Quilts Formally Donated to MAQS
  Bill and Meredith Schroeder and Schroeder Publishing quilts formally donated to MAQS to become the core of the Founders Collection. These quilts had previously been on loan to MAQS.

December 1997
Patchworks of Remembrance & Hope Project Launched
  In response to the December 1, 1997, shootings at Heath High

School in Paducah, KY, MAQS invited people around the world to create 12" quilt blocks and write short narratives to communicate their feelings.

September 1998
First Quilt-a-Thon Held at MAQS
Quilters gather to complete Patchworks of Hope & Remembrance. Quilters continue to gather annually for a Quilters for Charity Day.

December 1999
MAP II Survey Completed
The museum underwent an American Association of Museum "Collections Management Assessment." This is the second stage in moving the museum toward AAM accreditation.

February 2000
National Collection Advisory Committee Established
Following this committee's first meeting, the museum's campaign to add 10 quilts for 10 years to the collection was launched. Those ten quilts were added to the collection on March 1, 2001, and are included in this publication.

March 2000
MAQS Hosts a Tribute Exhibit and Gathering for the Late Doreen Speckmann

June 2000
MAQS Web Site is Launched at www.quiltmuseum.org

August 2000
U.S. Secretary of Education Riley Visits MAQS

2001
10th Anniversary of MAQS

August 2002
MAQS Begins 8-month Educational Outreach Project

May 2003
Patricia J. Morris Educational Fund Established

March 2004
Prize-Winning Quilters & Their Quilts: AQS 20th Anniversary Exhibition Opens

May 2004
Board of Directors Long Range Planning Retreat to Refine MAQS Goals and Objectives

August 2004
Kitty Shadle Volunteer Fund Established

Close Up_____

World attention was drawn to Paducah, Kentucky, on December 1, 1997, when shootings at Paducah's Heath High School left the community stunned. Out of that tragedy grew a MAQS project that had a profound impact on the museum's staff and community. Within a week, MAQS announced its Patchworks for Remembrance & Hope project, which invited anyone who wanted to create a 12" block for a quilt. In all, over 375 blocks from around the world arrived and they were made into 27 quilts, which were displayed in December 1998.

TOP: **Wayne Bates has demonstrated annually since the first Arts in Action festival in 1996. In 2000 the October event sponsored by Paducah Bank drew over 10,000 visitors.**

MIDDLE: **Installation of the political exhibit curated by Julie and Robin Powell which was on display in 1996 during President Clinton's campaign stop in Paducah. On the left is Ed Larson's quilt CLINTON WINS.**

BOTTOM: **U.S. Secretary of Education Richard Riley addressing an audience in the MAQS galleries, with the P&B Textiles sponsored MAQS School Block Challenge 2000 winning blocks behind him.**

MAQS Collection
Index

MAQS COLLECTION QUILTS

Aletsch 74, 75
Air Show 14, 15
Amish Easter Baskets 58, 59
Amish Mutual Aid 52, 53
Ancient Directions 76, 77
Ann Orr's "Ye Olde Sampler" . . . 44, 45
Autumn Radiance 36, 37
Baltimore Remembered 34
Barking Up the Wrong Tree 96
Basket of Flowers 8, 40
Baskets and the Corn 86, 87
Baskets I 60, 61
Beach Roses 24, 25
Beatles Quilt, The 82, 83
Bed of Peonies 64, 65
Beginnings, The 72
Birds of a Different Color 50
Blade, The 54, 55
Blazing Splendor 42, 43
Blue Earth Filled with Water and Flowers . 98, 99
Blueberry Morning 101
Boat in a Bottle Sampler 20, 21
Brown County Log Cabins 24, 25
Buffalo Magic 40, 41
Butternut Summer 80, 81
Cabins in the Cosmos 94
Celebration 84
Celebration of Autumn 16, 17
Cherry Rose 30
Chips and Whetstones 32
Cityscape 18, 19
Clamshell 68, 69
Colonial Lady 68, 69
Community Barn Raising 24, 25
Complimentary Composition 101
Conway Album (I'm Not from
        Baltimore) 19, 38, 39
Corn Crib 18
Corona II: Solar Eclipse 76, 77
Country Garden 56, 57
Country School 36, 37
Crossings 92, 93
Crown of Cerise 32, 33
Dawn Splendor 22
Descending Visions 40
Desert Dusk 14, 15
Designer Christmas Trees 48, 49
Diffractions III 92
Discovery 82, 83
Distant Closeness 74, 75
Dot's Vintage 1983 . . . . 62, 63
Double Wedding Ring 56, 57
Dreamcatcher 46, 47
Dresden Garden 96
Enlightenment 98, 99
Escapade 83
Escape from Circle City 22, 23
Fear of the Dark 80, 81
Feathered Friends 40, 41

Feathered Star Bouquet 42, 43
Feathered Star Sampler 56
Floral Urns 80, 81
Flower Basket 86, 87
Flower Basket Sampler 58, 59
Freedom's Cascade 20, 21
Galaxy of Quilters 18, 19
Garden Maze 18, 19
Garden Party 42, 43
Goato and Friends 78, 79
Grace 84
Grandmother's Engagement Ring (Statz) . . . 16
Grandmother's Engagment Ring (Sepulvado) 48, 49
Great American Elk 86, 87
Gypsy in My Soul 70, 71
Hammered at Home 78, 79
Hearts & Stars 88, 89
Heliacal Rise 78, 79
Here Between 26, 27
Hot Fun 76, 77
Ice Fantasia 26, 27
Incantation 90, 91
Indian Barn Raising 98, 99
Indiana Crazy 88, 89
Indian Summer 78, 79
It's Not Summer Yet 100
Javanese Jungle 36
Jelly Bean 86, 87
Joie de Vie – Joy of Life 62, 63
Kettle Moraine Star 78, 79
Lancaster County Rose 42, 43
Le Jardin de Nos Reves 66, 67
Li'l Bit Crazy Two, A 51
Lilies Are Forever 66, 67
Lilies of Autumn 46, 47
Lime Light 101
Listen to Your Mother 20
Little Bit of Candlewicking, A 90, 91
Looking Back on Broken Promises . . . 26, 27
Maltese Cross 68, 69
Mandala of Flowers, A 91
Many Stars 95
Maple Leaf 16, 17
Map Makers, The 12
Mariner's Compass 54, 55
May Shadows 42
Midwinter Night's Dream 60, 61
Migration #2 . . . . 92, 93
Momma's Garden 30, 31
Morisco 72, 73
Morning Glory 34, 35
Mother's Day 100
Mount Pleasant Miners 28, 29
Mountain and the Magic:
        Night Lights, The 26
Move Over Matisse I 30, 31
Mount St Helens, Did You Tremble? . . . 26, 27
Na Pali 16, 17
Nature's Walk 38, 39
Ne'er Encounter Pain 68, 69
Neon Nights 88, 89
New Directions 48
New York Beauty 52, 53
Night and Noon Variation 72, 73
Night Beacons III 92
Night Bloom 62, 63
Night Flowers 74, 75

Nosegay 66, 67
Nothing Gold Can Stay 54, 55
October Morning 80, 81
Oh My Stars 62, 63
Ohio Bride's Quilt 76
Olde English Medallion 58, 59
On Wednesday Morning 28, 29
One Fish, Two Fish, Red Fish, Blue Fish . 82, 83
Orchard Beauty 38, 39
Oriental Fantasy 32, 102
Oriental Poppy 56, 57
Our Secret Garden 34
Outlooks 24
Pandas 'round the World 24, 25
Peace and Love 44, 45
Persian Paradise 44, 45
Phoenix Rising 34, 35
Pineapple Log Cabin 52, 53
Pop Stars 98, 99
Poppies & Other California Beauties . . 40, 41
Precipice 84, 85
President's Wreath Variation 36, 37
Progressive Pictorial Quilt, The 20, 21
Prosperity 60, 61
Quilted Counterpane 66, 67
Raggedy Sun Worshippers 18
Reach For the Stars 72, 73
Red Poppies 28, 29
Reflection #3 . . . . 94, 95
Restoring the Balance 74, 75
Ribbons and Roses 90, 91
Rising Moons 64, 65
Rococo Islands 66, 67
Rosemaling Inspiration 30, 31
Roses by Starlight 48, 49
Roses for a June Bride 44, 45
Saturn's Rings 70, 71
Serenity II: Life in My Pond 28, 29
Shadow Baltimore Bride 90, 91
Silversword – Degener's Dream 23
Snow Scape 97
Sophistication 16, 17
Space Quilt, The 102, 103
Spice of Life 102, 103
Splendor of the Rajahs 56, 57
Spring Flower Baskets 70, 71
Spring Winds 30, 31
Springtime Sampler 76
Square within a Square within
        a Square 58, 59
Stained Glass Windows 88, 89
Star Bright 64
Star of Chamblie 52, 53
Star-Crossed 50, 51
Star Flower 102
Starburst 55
Starry, Starry Night 60, 61
Stella Antigua 64, 65
Strawberry Sundae 72, 73
Submergence 46, 47
Sun-Bathing Blue Tit 102, 103
Sunburst Quilt 46, 47
Sunset Kites 52
Sweetheart on Parade 80, 81
Taos Tapestry 14, 15
Tennessee Pink Marble 64, 65
Terrarium 94

Other MAQS Exhibition *Publications*

These books can be found in the MAQS bookshop, 215 Jefferson St., Paducah, KY 42001, and in local bookstores and quilt shops. If you are unable to locate a title in your area, you can order:

on-line at
www.quiltmuseum.org

To order by Visa, Discover, or Mastercard call:
1-270-442-8856

American Quiltmaking: 1970–2000
Eleanor Levie
#6414: AQS, 2004, 144 pages, 8½" x 11", softbound, $25.95.

Bear's Paw: New Quilts from an Old Favorite
#5754: AQS, 2001, 96 pages, 8½" x 11", softbound, $19.95.

Editor's Choice: New Quilts from an Old Favorite Contest
#6078: AQS, 2002, 96 pages, 8½" x 11", softbound, $19.95.

Feathered Star: New Quilts from an Old Favorite
#6209: AQS, 2003, 96 pages, 8½" x 11", softbound, $21.95.

Kaleidoscope: New Quilts from an Old Favorite
#5296: AQS, 1999, 104 pages, 8½" x 11", softbound, $16.95.

Monkey Wrench: New Quilts from an Old Favorite
#6412: AQS, 2004, 96 pages, 8½" x 11", softbound, $21.95.

**Prize-Winning Quilters and Their Quilts:
AQS 20th Anniversary Exhibition**
Marjorie L. Russell
#6416: AQS, 2004, 48 pages, 8½" x 11", softbound, $14.95

Quilts by Paul D. Pilgrim: Blending the Old & the New
Gerald E. Roy
#4918: AQS, 1997, 80 pages, 8½" x 11", softbound, $16.95.

Seven Sisters: New Quilts from an Old Favorite
#6677: AQS, 2005, 96 pages, 8½" x 11", softbound, $21.95.

Storm at Sea: New Quilts from an Old Favorite
#5592: AQS, 2000, 96 pages, 8½" x 11", softbound, $19.95.

Tumbling Blocks: New Quilts from an Old Favorite
#6005: AQS, 2002, 96 pages, 8½" x 11", softbound, $19.95.